TO HEAVEN, WITH SCRIBES
AND PHARISEES

TO HEAVEN, WITH SCRIBES AND PHARISEES

The Jewish Path to God

LIONEL BLUE

New York
OXFORD UNIVERSITY PRESS
1976

First published in the United States of America
in 1976 by Oxford University Press, Inc.
200 Madison Avenue, New York, New York 10016

ISBN 0 19519831 X

Printed in the United States of America

Contents

Foreword

There were books, he said, on every type of spirituality – Hindus, Catholics, Buddhists and Orthodox were all displaying their spiritual treasures and people were buying them. But where, he insisted, were the Jews?

I thought of my friends and colleagues. In my mind, I took them away from their endless meetings, and dressed them in loincloths and cassocks, their faces turned to the Infinite.

It didn't fit.

He resumed. What about the Zohar? What about all these esoteric and exotic mystical traditions?

What about the Zohar! What about the workers indeed! I had never read through the Zohar myself, nor had anyone I knew. There was a Christian professor of mysticism of course, who might . . . But he wouldn't do, the wrong brand.

Then I thought of Jewish suffering, and Jewish jokes, all that had been endured without bitterness or hatred. And not by saints either but by ordinary Jewish people, the Cohens, and the Levys who live next door. Suddenly I wanted to tell how they got to heaven with all their relations, the Children of Israel.

I had always known their goodness, their spirituality if you like so well that I had never explained it even to myself, let alone to others.

I tried it on my non-Jewish friends, on Leslie Shepard, my teacher, on Gordian and Isidore, who were Dominicans, on Kim, who was a sort of Anglican, on Nicholas, who was a Carmelite and not least on the Sisters of Sion of 17 Chepstow Villas in London who listened very patiently.

This book is dedicated to them, and their goodwill.

LIONEL BLUE

TO HEAVEN, WITH SCRIBES
AND PHARISEES

Chapter One

Through the Looking Glass

The Rabbis say: If anyone comes nowadays, and desires to become a proselyte, they say to him 'Why do you want to become a proselyte? Do you not know that the Israelites are harried, hounded, persecuted, and harassed, and that sufferings befall them?' If he says: 'I know it, and I am not worthy', they receive him without further argument.

Talmud Yebamot

Rab said: A man will have to give account in the judgement day of every good thing which he might have enjoyed and did not.

Jerusalem Talmud Kiddushin

It is not possible to meet with Jewish spirituality without meeting Jews, and Jews may not be immediately likable. In the Western world they live mainly in the dormitory suburbs of the great towns. They are highly literate, and middle-class. They are small tradesmen, professional men, dentists and accountants, heavily involved in property, entertainment and trade. They do not incline to asceticism but to politics, and they are deeply involved in the material world. They have produced both the great socialists, and the great capitalists of our time. Their greatest characteristics are vitality and hope. In this century a third of their number were exterminated, but within a decade the remnant that survived produced a semi-messianic state.

This deep involvement with materialism can be profoundly shocking to anyone with a 'spiritual' idea of religion. Many Christians have found it uncomfortable. Belloc disliked it; so did Chesterton, and Kierkegaard poured scorn on it. At first sight it does seem rather gross, and earthy, reflecting all the ills of an affluent society. Many Christians have tried to ignore this material involvement of Judaism. They approach such Jewish works as the Talmud, wanting to learn about Jewish spirituality, and all they find are endless discussions about property rights, divorce settlements, and such punishments as stoning, strangling, burning and beheading. The last are particularly bewildering, as the death penalty has not been current in Judaism for 2000 years. Many Jews play the same game of theological hide-and-seek, as they try to give Judaism a Christian face-lift before presenting it to the world. In this light Jesus becomes a Pharisee, with liberal tastes, and the mystical rabbis of Eastern Europe become conventional saints, though 'saint' is a foreign idea to the world of Judaism. An ecumenical result is achieved, but there has been a cheating for the best of motives, and a pious dishonesty. The disembowelled Judaism which emerges would be barely adequate for a backward youngster, let alone for a complex intellectual, and there are many of the latter in Judaism.

To enter the inner world of the Jewish religion requires therefore an initial stripping, a deliberate unlearning of what religion is about, and a new definition of words. It means detachment from the beloved myths and stories which helped many to spiritual progress, but which can only wither in the desert winds which blow even through the modern satisfied Jewish society of the suburbs. To a Christian this is especially difficult, as Judaism forces him to stand outside his own tradition, to see it through the looking glass. The two religions have been too closely related to admit of any easy cocktail-party solutions. Too much blood has flowed, too much persecution has occurred, too much libel and too much love turned sour.

Why should this stony road be pursued? Perhaps because God likes stony roads more than primrose ones, for according to Christians He Himself has said it. Where the hurt is greater the reconciliation must be deeper. The discipline involved prevents us from the most dangerous of religious temptations – lacking respect for reality as it is, and inventing an artificial, expurgated one to which we can apply our simplified answers. Religious truth,

after all, has an acid, stinging, hurtful quality; religious senti-
mentality has not.

It also seems in our time as if the will of God drives us to
encounter 'the other', to make contact with other holy ghettos who
are involved with the same realities. The first 'other' that we encounter is the other sitting on our doorstep. It is not difficult to
feel warm say to Lao-Tse, because we do not have to live next
door to his disciples, smell their cooking, and endure their different way of life. Encountering Judaism means encountering
Jews. No matter how lofty the ideal, how profound the mysticism, both are fused into the living flesh and blood of the Cohens
and Levys one meets in daily life – our difficult neighbours, but
according to their own lights a holy nation and a kingdom of
priests. This encounter with Judaism teaches us one great truth –
human minds can create theology but God's supreme creation
was not an idea, but the living flesh and blood which could accept
or reject Him. With Judaism we do not encounter a philosophy
or ideology, but the will of God alive in a group of human beings,
with all its potentiality for tragedy and joy.

Yet another reason for the search! The forms of the Jewish
religion are more relevant to Western society now than at any
other time. We live in a world of uneasy affluence, involved in
the material things around us. The cars, and the freezers, and the
country retreats have become extensions of our personalities.
Unfortunately religion tends to be romantic, and does not
assimilate such things. It is traditionally more at home with a
rural scene, the simple life and classic forms of charity and service – saintly men who offer cloaks to beggars. It has difficulty in
turning away from classical problems of poverty and persecution
to the modern problems of leisure, affluence, and the permissive-
ness they bring. As a result religious groups play safe. They
scavenge the world for problems which admit of classical solutions. They have much to say about the third world, which is
conveniently far, but little about the society to which they minister.
This gives them all an odd sense of unreality.

Judaism is not a difficult religion to understand, but it is a
difficult one to explain. Ask a Jew about Jewish spirituality, or

Judaism itself, and he will stammer out an answer, or be tongue-tied – an odd reaction for such an articulate people. He may offer an haphazard though fairly accurate list of practices, or a wildly inaccurate statement of beliefs. He will be at a loss, because he has probably never consciously thought about Judaism, he will only have felt it and experienced it. How can one describe a taste, a flavour, or the inner echoes of a Yiddish joke? Is it possible to make a theology out of Jewish humour, or be consistent about a culture which has been touched by every tradition of Europe, Asia, and America? Jews have not, after all, chosen to be Jewish. They have not inspected the religious alternatives of the world, prodded them for spirituality and juiciness and selected the best buy. Their experience is the opposite. They didn't choose to be Jewish, God seems to have prodded and chosen them, and there is nothing they can do about it.

To describe something, means to be outside it, and Judaism is not a religion for outsiders. For centuries it has been an island, a beleaguered fortress in a hostile world, and the drawbridge has been up. Jews have lived for centuries beside their Christian cousins. They were present in Germany before the Germans, they wrote in Spanish (in Hebrew letters, of course) before Spain was even a dream. But they lived, so to speak, on another planet. The gentile world around them was as distant as the moon, and equally remote and cold. To ask a Jew about his spirituality is to ask a Jew a Christian question. All he can do is to stammer out a defective Christian answer.

Jews no longer missionise or convert, though they did so once and all modern Jews are descended from converts of former times. Judaism nearly conquered the Roman world. Ladies at Nero's court kept the kosher food laws. There was a Jewish empire in the middle ages which stretched from Moscow to the Black Sea. Small Iberian towns had a dozen or more synagogues. Poles, Russians, Ukranians, and Lithuanians quarrelled over the identity of whole towns or villages. They were all right and all wrong, because the disputed territories were inhabited by Jews, who spoke all their languages and were identified with none of them. Nevertheless Jews have not been missionaries for a long time. Perhaps because they did not want to, perhaps because they were not allowed to. Until recently if a Jew converted a Christian, both converter and convertee could be burnt to death. In modern times a nobleman suffered this fate in Poland. The deterrent was effective and Jews not unnaturally got out of the habit. This has intensified their theological inwardness. They have not been used to explaining their religious experience to outsiders. They have had little practice at it. Being a hospitable people, they will short-circuit the request, and invite the enquirer to a Sabbath meal or to a Jewish wedding. They will not be wrong. They will merely have altered the question. The enquirer is asking for a Jewish creed, but he will be offered a Jewish experience instead.

There is another problem which is even more difficult to explain. It is not easy for a Jew to pin his Judaism down. Does he give an account of his grandparents' religion? The religion of the old country was medieval but it was certainly consistent. Unfortunately it has one great defect, it is not there any longer, and only returns in the waves of nostalgia which periodically overwhelm the Jewish world. His own Judaism has been smashed too many times to be nicely packaged for export. It probably migrated from Eastern Europe to the West. It has journeyed from a closed to an open society. It has witnessed the destruction of European Jewry, the collapse of liberal hopes and the rise of Israel. Every particle of it has been shaken, and the particles have barely settled in the uneasy peace which has followed the Second World War. They have little shape, these particles of tradition and memory, but they have been burnt into his flesh and they will cling to him throughout his life. What is their spirituality? A Jew cannot say – he only knows that their strength is beyond reason, and their power different from any other in the world.

Persecution and uneasy toleration have broken the old world of the Pharisees. One Jewish world has come to an end and another has scarcely begun. Jews live in the untidy workshop out of which a new Judaism is being born. The majority of Jews have abandoned large tracts of Jewish law, and it is unlikely that they will ever return. The Zohar – the classic of Jewish mysticism – is scarcely read, and the Talmud is for experts. The wind of God has changed direction. Who knows where it will blow His people now? It may be that the era of synagogues and rabbis is ending, as the era of the Temple also ended. Jews are borne along by a greater emotion than nostalgia, and that is hope. They are not merely pushed from Sinai, so many thousands of years behind them, but they are also pulled to the revelation which lies ahead. At this point in the journey it is well to look back to the Jewish life which has just gone by. It was the work of the scribes and the Pharisees, who argued with Jesus in the synagogue (and also with each other). This book will describe their special path to God, to which they remained loyal through every persecution. By understanding them a Christian will gain a new perspective on Jesus. He will cease to be an icon, but will step back into Jewish history, into the framework of Jewish life, which was his home.

Chapter Two

Earning a Living in the Cosmos

A favourite saying of the Rabbis of Yavneh was:
I am God's creature and my fellow is God's creature.
My work is in the town and his work is in the country.
I rise early for my work and he rises early for his work.
Just as he does not presume to do my work, so I do not presume
to do his work.
Will you say, I do much and he does little?
We have learnt: One may do much or one may do little;
It is all one, provided he directs his heart to heaven.

Talmud Berachot

At the centre of Judaism is a revelation, and this revelation is recorded in five books. They are written on a scroll, and the scroll is kept in the Ark of a Jewish synagogue. This scroll is the heart of Judaism. All Jewish literature is only one vast commentary on it. Imagine then a cross-section of a tree. The innermost ring is the Torah – the teaching, the Law – and around it cluster ring after ring of commentary and argument, as each generation adds its own life experience to the formative experience of the people.

It is not easy to say what exactly happened, because language is good when it talks about objects such as pots and pans; it stammers when it tries to communicate deeper experience, such as great love; and it is inadequate when it tries to talk about such things as a meeting with infinity, or appointments with destiny. 'Revelation' is not a good term, as it is not really a Jewish word at all. According to the Torah, which is the result and record of the experience, 'God came down,' and intervened.

He did not come down like a theatrical prop, because He (It or She) is beyond space and time. Modern writers pooh-pooh the idea of a human figure in the sky; the writers of the Bible used such images (one can't think without images) but always went beyond them. Anyway, Infinity, God or 'X', if you like, came down and met a small bedouin tribe, accompanied by a mixed bag of hangers-on. The encounter was explosive, this bedouin family was hurled into history, to great glory and terrible suffering.

All Jews, when they try to explain themselves, and understand themselves, which they don't find easy, turn back to the five books of Moses written on the scroll. These five books are not Judaism's last word, but they are Judaism's centre. They don't talk about the after-life, or the messiah, and it is no use searching them for a theology. If you insist on the attempt, you might find none, or you might find several (which is I suppose the same thing). There are some beautiful thoughts, like 'You should love your neighbour as yourself', but one can't call them pretty books, or a collection of pious texts. This disappoints many Jews today, when they go to synagogue. They would prefer something less craggy, with more piety and feeling. The Torah records occasional religious experiences grandly but laconically, and does not dwell on them. (There are not many lines about the burning bush, for example.) It gives a sketch of the early history of the people, and is so painfully honest that it does not suppress the warts, nor divide people into goodies or baddies. It is a relief, after the hero-worship of the twentieth century, and the byzantine adjectives, the educated have heaped on Hitler, Stalin, Mao and other passing politicians, to turn to an account of Moses which includes his temper and his stammer, to Jacob and his cheating, to the matriarchs and their scheming, and the fairness and decency of the arch-opponent Esau, who got left out of the divine history.

Even religious history is not the main interest of the Torah. Its real interest is taxes, social welfare, communual organisation, inheritance, crime, authority, and procedure. Above all, it is passionately interested in detail. Even when dealing with objects of piety such as the Tabernacle it doesn't go off into homily, allegory, or other pious pursuits. Instead it gets enthusiastic about measurements, materials, and their costing. These are given with all the accuracy a pre-technological people can muster.

God pokes his nose into all the nooks and crannies of life. There are laws about birds' nests, and shopping-scales, infectious diseases and care of the environment. It doesn't seem spiritual, because it is so tremendously involved in the material world. Only occasionally are we reminded that the source of this passion for matter is not material. The Power which calls us to work in the world is itself 'apart' unworldly, and holy ('holy' in Hebrew, in fact, means something which is apart, which is different). The nature of the 'apartness' and its identity is glimpsed in the burning bush, in Jacob's dream, or in the exchange between It and Moses at Mount Sinai.

'It' may be at rest and beyond change, but Its commandments are terse, staccato, and pushy. 'Do this!' says the Torah. 'Do this!' or 'Don't do that!' says the Torah. 'Don't do that!' – this is its typical statement. There isn't much time for religious experience because there is literally too much to do, and everyone is caught on the hop. Judaism is not a theology, and not a system of piety. God did not reveal Himself in this way at the meeting. Judaism is a task, an activity, and work is the key to it. One commandment follows another (there are no less than 613), and religion means, in the first instance, doing them, not contemplating them or praying them, or bowing down in front of them, or philosophising about them, or kissing them.

For a Jew, work may not be the centre of God's religion, but it is the centre of his. (God and man have different natures, and different interests – they are not the same.) The universe is not there to do our will, but we are there to help it along. Work and business are holy matters, for creation is not in a state of rest. It too is working out a purpose, and we are part of it. Like any other creature we do not exist for ourselves, but we have to earn our living in the cosmos. For Jews there is an exhilaration in doing this work, and real pleasure comes from earning one's living. We feel the surge of the spirit, as we rush from committee to committee, from activity to activity, working for the Kingdom of God (or, if you want, the republic of goodness).

Every religious person tries to describe his relationship to God, the link which connects him to the unseen source of power. Christians are part of the body of Christ. They are part of him, and he is one with his Father. Jews do not stress this relationship so much, this family feeling with the Almighty, they assume it, but use it more cautiously, and with less vivid illustrations. The language of Jewish spirituality has a different look for those unaccustomed to it. Although God is our Father, in daily life it is often better to think of Him as our Employer. According to the Jewish commentaries and readings of Isaiah, the Children of Israel firmly state what is the best terminology for their religious purpose. 'Do not call us your children,' they cry, 'call us your builders!' Jews describe themselves as 'employees', and God as the 'Employer'. They go even further. They use language which is as daring in its way as the language about the body of Christ for a Christian. They talk about themselves as 'co-partners with God, in the work of creation'. The details of all this are spelt out and they need no apology or gloss. God is 'faithful to pay our wages', says the Talmud. And it adds: 'the interest on good deeds can be enjoyed in this world' and, wonder of wonders – ' the capital remains intact for us in the world to come'.

It is important to realise that Judaism has no hankering for feudal ideals, or for aesthetic republics, like Plato. It is unashamedly bourgeois, and middle-class in its preoccupations. Like other religions it is concerned with poverty. It does not, however, glorify that state, it would like to end it. The Jewish servants of God in this world are not perfect knights, or lonely hermits, but the holy company of righteous businessmen, the pious organisers of communities, the committee men, and *apparatchiks* who give their time and energy freely; the heroes who attend to the details of the world, and keep it going, for it does not go round by itself. As they do their holy work, the holiness rubs off on them, and makes them holy too. Provided they are working for God, and not for their own glory or ambition, this is their path to salvation. Over the concentration camp entrance the

Nazis hung a sign, '*Arbeit macht Frei*' (work makes free). This was terrible because it distorted a truth which is one of the deepest in Jewish experience – the salvation, to which daily work honestly done, is the door.

The material world we live in is not only the place of our work, it is the material we work with. No artist, no craftsman, can despise his own tools, and the medium he works in. No Jew can ever really deplore or despise the world. It can irritate him and hurt him, but he cannot reject it. Even wanting to do so would be irreligious. It is where God put us, where we have to earn our living. When we have done this, but not before, we can turn to other realities, and worlds which certainly exist. Until then, it is better not to dwell on them, except as compass points for finding our way. They are the joys of a religious retirement, which most of us have yet to earn. In the meantime we get on with the job.

The job is described in a work called *The Prepared Table* written in the sixteenth century by a rabbi called Joseph Karo. It is 'Prepared' because he digested the tangled mass of the Talmud, the continuing arguments and discussions, the holy clash of opinion, and set out the results so lucidly, so clearly, that, as he says, even a fool, or a child or (I apologise) a housewife could come to the table, to find the will of God and eat without intellectual indigestion. This is the indispensable book for traditional Judaism, and a work of art. Karo was himself one of the inner circle of Jewish mystics. Whatever his own personal inspiration (he had a spirit guide), this never diverted him from the small things of the world, and the almost pedantic accuracy, with which they have to be considered.

The work lies all around us. We work in the world outside us and also in the other very real world that lies within us. We stand still, but every part of us, every cell, is working. We go to work, to an office or factory, and we work to unite this world to the unchanging reality that lies beyond it. With our conscience we sew them together. The work can be approached at any angle, or in any way. It is a whole, and one part always leads to another. If we deny its complexity, we become lop-sided, and then dangerous and futile. Many want to work only in the external world, but not on themselves. They want to make reality more tractable, and easier to manipulate. Their work then turns into manipulation. They manipulate each other and themselves. They cannot solve the world's problems, but only reflect them.

There are others who evade in different ways. They push aside the external world, and use piety as a refuge. They are so absorbed in their own spiritual systems that they are subtly side-tracked back into the ego. When evil and corruption stalk the world they do not see it, they are so busy looking for dust specks in their inner tidy pious rooms. They may have tasted the joys of heaven, but they have not earned their living in the cosmos. In Jewish eyes, they can be a spiritual success, but a religious failure. This was the pitfall of many pious people between the two world wars.

Which work is higher, which work is lower? Who knows! Each one of us is given his own work, and until we have done it, this is the highest for us. The laws of the Torah are not the most ethereal, nor the most poetical, but they are the ones God has set for his people. Which is more needed, earthly love or mystical love? The former at least makes the world go round, and ensures that mystics are born!

Rabbi Shimon Ben Yochai, the traditional founder of Kabbalah, had to change the order of his priorities sharply. After his years of contemplation in a cave, following the defeat in the wars against Rome, he came out only to see people ploughing and sowing seed, instead of studying Torah. He shouted out to them that this was no time for such trivialities. But the Lord Himself intervened, and ordered Rabbi Shimon to go back into his cave, until he realised the importance of the seemingly trivial things that make the world go round. Judaism does not encourage snobbery of a mystical kind.

There is another story about the greatest rabbi of his time – Elijah, the Gaon of Vilna. In the eighteenth century the learned rabbi was giving a tutorial. Two of his pupils looked out of the window at a bird soaring in the sky. He asked one of them, 'What were you thinking, as you watched the bird?' 'I was thinking of the soul ascending to heaven,' the boy replied. Elijah thought, and asked him to leave his class. He smelt the mysticism of Jewish Poland. He turned to the other boy, and asked him the same question. The boy considered. 'If that bird dropped dead, and fell between two fences,' he said, 'who would own the body?' His teacher replied, 'God be praised, for someone knows what religion is about!'

Christian piety is worrying to many Jews, precisely because it is so attractive. But it seems too religious to be Jewish. There is more cake than daily bread in the diet, and a Jew gets worried by spiritual indigestion. It is heady stuff, for the pupils of scribes and Pharisees. It is easy to get drunk on it, if one is not used to it, and if we get drunk how can we do our duty, and deal with the details of life – the fences, the quarrels, and the committees which we were sent to sanctify? For Jews religious experience can lead away from the religious duty to which God called us, and for which He gave us so many laws and commandments.

The centre of Judaism is therefore not a creed nor a theology, nor even an experience – the Torah knows little of such things – but a task! Its unity does not come from an orthodoxy, where we all believe the same things, but from an orthopraxis, where we all work together for the same things. Occasionally Jews would like to be religiously respectable, i.e., like Christians, and books and sermons appear telling them what to believe. They look solid enough on the outside, not very different from Christian or Marxist textbooks on the same lines. But the outsider should beware! If the book is consistent and dogmatic, he should look at the reviews. The definer of Judaism is found to live in glorious isolation, the sole inhabitant of his own orthodox fortress. If the book truly reflects the reality of Judaism, in its richness, its confusion and its urgency, so many theological theories will be presented, so many alternatives about suffering, about the messianic kingdom, and about the after-life, that the reader will turn away bewildered. This diversity is typical of all Jews including Jesus. He spoke little theology. He asked for certain things to be done, and for certain realities to be recognised. His sayings and parables are the stuff upon which theo-

23

logies can rest, they are not a theology in themselves. He was not a theologian because he was a Jew. His later followers, who were not Jews, expressed those realities in terms of theology.

The holiness of work and the urgency of it is the guide through the jungle of detailed law, planted and shaped by the scribes and Pharisees. Everything that existed in the Torah was intensified in them. It was not enough to state the principles, like the prophets. It was necessary to put them into action and administer them from an office, decide their detail in a law court, and implement them by community pressure. 'Righteousness, righteousness you shall pursue', says Moses. The Deuteronomist (for cognoscenti of Biblical Criticism) and the scribes and Pharisees carried the pursuit into every detail of human life. They tried to build a holy and righteous society, wherever they were, and so do we their descendants. No environment can release us from this task. It is done in the squalor of a ghetto, in the blankness of a modern suburb, or even in a concentration camp. We are not released by any situation.

As time went on, the passion for detail of the scribes and Pharisees became even stronger. The workmen were now settling down to the job! As they built the Kingdom of Heaven in miniature, they had to consider each brick and each pebble. Today we, their last descendants, also ask, what is God's will in relation to the details of our life, to our property, to our love-making, to our kitchen equipment, to our contracts, gossip, gambling and to our quarrels. These are not pious subjects, but these fill the Talmud and all the commentaries which surround it. There are beautiful thoughts in these books but they lie alongside argumentative thoughts, disturbing thoughts, and some very nasty thoughts. A Christian should not be shocked. The Psalter he uses has the same characteristics. Both are Jewish books, with a deep respect for life as it is, for us as we are, and for the world as God has made it. Both prefer reality unexpurgated. They gain in zest what they lack in spirituality.

For Judaism the Kingdom of God on earth is designed for human beings as they are, and not as they might be. We work with, and for what exists, not for yearnings or wish fulfilment. It is this which draws us near to our close relatives, the Marxists. For they too work hard and are in love with a righteous society, though not with a holy one. A Jewish passion goes through them too. Our present quarrel with them is not a cold one, or a detached one, for we share the same love. It has the fierceness of a family quarrel. No people gave more to its political ideals than the Jews, and one of the most glorious chapters in our history is that of the Jewish martyrs for materialism. It is a deep wound that these workers for righteousness ended in the labour camps, disappeared in the last days of Stalin, or were judicially murdered in the purges which erased all that could still question, and be open to the spirit. Jews always pose a question to the cultures in which they live. They work too hard, they talk too much, and they don't quite fit. People want fake security; they want the world to stand still. But Jews are restless like the world, and move on, shaking the bureaucracies and official structures, the dominions and thrones, a disturbing element in the life of the world. The Kingdom of God requires both destruction and creation. God is a workman, and we are the tools of His trade. The great sin of a tool, of an instrument, and therefore of the Jewish people, is to be idle.

Does it matter that they are atheists, and we are not? The question was asked by a traditional rabbi, 'Why was atheism created?' He answered, 'So that we should not rely only on God, when we work in the world, but carry on as if He did not exist, and the responsibility was on our shoulders alone.'

We can put things in the hands of God, it is true, but this is small satisfaction, for we are His hands, His instruments in the world. We do the work badly, or we do it well, but the work goes on, and we are part of it.

As Jews therefore, there is a bond which links us to all who work at dreams, and who plan and plot for the coming of the Kingdom. Our sympathy goes out to dreamers who do their homework, who have a passion for detail as the Torah commands, who not only talk in cafés and common-rooms, but also go on to implement it, and continue the work of creation. We share the excitement of all the builders of Utopia. A religious bond connects us to the Utopians, the anarchists, the reformers, the cooperators and the collectivists. They are as close to us in their way as Christians, for among all religious people we Jews are the holy materialists, loving and respecting the matter out of which we were fashioned, and knowing that unless we approach it in holiness, we shall misuse it, and deform the world. Work, then, dominates the Jewish world. Activity is its characteristic whether in a suburb or in a Jewish state. Neither are in a state of rest, both are busy-busy, and this is their tradition. Hillel said we should never separate ourselves from the community, but sometimes we have to stand outside it, in order to see it as it is, and the role of work within the community. Jews use work in three ways, to sanctify themselves, to protect themselves from themselves and other people, and to avoid God in themselves. It is used to meet God and evade Him at the same time.

The legitimate uses of work have been described, but the modern crisis in Judaism is not a crisis of work. The crisis is one of purpose, i.e. what do we work for and what is the purpose of our action? Our problem is not the six working days, but the seventh day of rest. Many Jews find that their holidays are the difficulty. This is a personal expression of a deep malaise in Jewish society. Work for Jews has a therapeutic function. It is a way to overcome bitterness, to cope with intense suffering and disaster. Its roots lie deep in the heart of Rabbinic Judaism. In times of trouble the Jewish response was effective and obvious. It was to increase the number of commandments, in other words work was used to overcome fear and insecurity. This reaction has its positive and negative sides. The response to the Second World War indicates both. After the external insecurity had ended, the internal traumas were still there. Jews overcame this by the spectacular creation of Israel. It is almost impossible to conceive the work, the activity, and the talent, which went to make the state. Whatever it merits and its failures, the work itself was the Jewish way to psychic health. In Europe, in a less obvious but impressive fashion, the inmates of the concentration camps patiently created new businesses, and in a short time, the scars of the holocaust were scarcely visible.

Israel works, it is a going concern. So do the Jewish suburbs. But what should they work towards? An idealised social welfare state is not enough, and the restoration of the Temple is hardly credible, and in its old form scarcely desirable. A young Jewish generation released from the perpetual crisis which its elders endured can not just work in response to sporadic emergencies. It may have to go beyond work and law, and Israel, to an encounter with God. It is only in His light that the great questions of Judaism can be resolved : What is the purpose of our work, what does the law require of us in our time, and what should we make out of Israel?

Chapter Three

The Lord of Hosts in Suburbia

The Jewish people, the separated people, therefore the holy people, is a God-made people. In our nobility and in our shabbiness, in our cultural refinement and in our vulgarity, in our endurance and in our weakness, in our glory and in the shame of our de-humanisation in Auschwitz – we are the people of God. . . . We did not choose to be Jews, God has chosen us.

Ignaz Maybaum

The Torah was not given to angels.

Talmud Berachot

A Jewish suburb looks ordinary enough. Its architecture is undistinguished, and there are not many signs that here God's chosen people are building His Kingdom on earth. It seems humdrum and materialist, engrossed in its own comfort and its own life. The food in the shops is richer than usual and there are more stores devoted to furs, jewellery, clothes, and the good life. It seems a long way from the Almighty, the El Shaddai, who led his people through the desert storms.

Nevertheless the traces of His presence are visible, if you want to see them. The kosher sign hangs outside shops. It adorns the rich salt beef of the restaurant. If your eyes are good enough, you will probably see a small notice in the clothing stores that you can get a kosher suit too, for a small extra payment. Kosher applies to more things than meat. There is an air of business and bustle in the suburb, a man goes by with a brief-case, intent and absorbed. Because hair is worn longer now, his side curls seem less exotic than in former times, though they owe little to fashion.

His black silk coat gives him an important look. What is he? The collector of synagogue dues? Not really! He is a follower of the great Jewish mystic who lived in Poland in the eighteenth century, who sought God in the solitude of the Carpathian mountains, but discovered Him in the joy of his own heart. He does not seem very joyous, you'd exclaim. Ah! but wait till you see him in the synagogue, dancing, and swaying with the Scroll – that's when his spiritual ascent is visible.

And that woman passing him wearing a wig, a rich chestnuty affair. She is doing it not for her own vanity, but for the sake of the Almighty. Indeed, all the oddities of Jewish life reflect the strangeness of God's will. There is no detail He has not interfered with, nothing without His imprint. What is that bread in the shops, plaited like a pigtail? It is the last remnant of the shewbreads which remained after the destruction of Jerusalem, and came to rest in bakers' shops. The little metal cases on the surrounds of Jewish doors are useful to Jewish charity collectors, who use them to spot likely donors. Their origin, however, is in one of the last speeches of Moses, when he was torn by anxiety, lest his people should forget what their own eyes had seen. Once you begin God-spotting in the Jewish suburb, you see Him everywhere. There is nothing His presence has not touched or moulded. In a corner of a room a piece of plaster has fallen away. It seems odd, for the room looks so newly decorated. The plaster was never there at all. Its absence reminds the satisfied occupants, who have taken so much trouble with the furniture and drapes, of the tragedies of their people. It reminds them even in their affluence that this room is part of a passing show, and that real home is elsewhere, not in another suburb, nor even in another country, but in another world.

In order to remember we tie knots in handkerchiefs. The Pharisees and rabbis tied knots everywhere, and in everything. The kitchen utensils, the salt beef, the silk coat, all point upwards beyond the logic of the world to their Creator. The problem for the religious tourist is that the Jewish surburb does not seem very grand. It is quite interesting and odd, but neither spiritual nor beautiful. The little groups of chattering men and women dressed to kill, on their way to and from synagogue, don't seem to have the inner glow of those who approach, or come away from a mystical experience or a communion. Because of this, it is very easy to misunderstand this little world and I must give a word of advice to the outsider, who may be Christian, or in our own times even Jewish.

A Christian should remember that though this world is strange to him, it was not strange to Jesus and the apostles, who would have recognised it. Jesus never ate non-kosher food in his life, and his clothing would have passed every test in the kosher-suit laboratory. (Yes, it really does exist – they make many cuts to test the fibres. After it passes the tests, it is pronounced kosher; whether it is wearable, I do not know!) The talking groups, and the arguments on the way to the Sabbath service, would have been very familiar to Jesus. Indeed, it is the only form of service where He and His disciples would have felt at home and whose prayers they would have known by heart. Like most Jews, He liked parties, and was interested in food. Jews like marriage feasts and wine and are much addicted to fatted calves. Jesus worked within the feelings of the Jewish world. Walk through a Jewish suburb. On a Friday night the candles are lit in Jewish homes. Look upwards! There in an upper room of a Jewish flat a man is blessing the bread and wine, and giving it to his family to eat!

Most Jews today also find their own suburbs perplexing, for there has been a break in their tradition. The knots are still there, and Jews still tie them, but few are sure what they are reminders of. Judaism as a result becomes a religion of knot-making for its own sake. Many Jews see the details, but not the reason for them, and without it the knots are certainly very odd indeed. Religion in this situation becomes a ragbag of old sociology, a curio shop full of religious antiques. The open society, the holocaust, and the great migrations have broken the traditions which stretched back to the days of Hillel, and even farther back to the time of Ezra, and possibly still farther back to the time of Moses, and Jewish prehistory. The behaviour patterns have remained, but their origins and their interior meaning have been lost in living memory. Judaism is a religion of insiders, difficult to assess by those

31

outside. The outsiders now, however, include possibly the majority of Jews.

It is obvious that the world of the Jewish suburb is a broken one, for the signs of decay are everywhere. In some shops, kosher has been replaced by 'Jewish-style' food – the rationale has changed from theology to gastronomy. Those who walk to 'shool' on the Sabbath pointedly ignore those who ride. Both feel uncomfortable with the even greater number who are going to have forbidden cups of coffee, in non-kosher cafés and coffee bars, profaning the Sabbath, and the mystery of creation it commemorates.

The Jewish community of London is an example; by hard work and talent and push, it has made a pilgrimage from the poverty of the East End to the comforts of Stamford Hill. From there it journeyed to the delights of Golders Green, and the euphoria of garden suburbs. On this journey to the good life, much of the old religious ballast has been jettisoned. Few would want to make the journey back any longer. Judaism is not a religion which encourages romantic attitudes, though it dabbles in nostalgia. But the journey has not been merely geographical, it has also been a journey through history and theology. A normal family in living memory, has travelled from medieval piety to enlightened materialism. Righteousness can survive the journey (there is no lack of advertisements for charity in the suburb), but holiness is a more delicate plant, and its survival is precarious. In many families milk and meat foods are traditionally kept apart. In the war the bombs came, and milk and meat dishes were blown into each other, and often never sorted out again. And for some families the complications of modern life are reflected in their refrigerator in an even odder fashion – there is a three-fold kitchen division – milk, meat and forbidden! To the outsider the attention which Judaism lavishes on food is excessive. But insiders know that the question of food involves, however clumsily, the meaning of ritual, the relevance of purity, and the survival of holiness. These details seem so small, almost trivial, but Judaism is a religion of detail. The scribes, Pharisees, and rabbis served God through detail. Out of small things, they created their master plan, for righteous and holy living.

Here lies a warning – do not approach Judaism with a non-Jewish mentality, for you will underrate it, or go away more puzzled than ever! Do not underrate details or put too much confidence in soaring abstractions! In Jewish experience God did not reveal Himself like that. If you excavate your way through the Torah, you will find 613 commandments, in a very puzzling order. There are many trees, but it is almost impossible to find the plan of the wood. There have been many attempts to elucidate and systematise this strange inheritance. Jewish intellect and Jewish genius have been devoted to this task for centuries; in the Mishnah, and Gemara of the rabbis, the 'Prepared Table' of Karo in the middle ages, and also the codes of Maimonides – the Jewish Aquinas – but none of them is a complete success. In fact, they have only made the wood even woodier. The original 613 have multiplied like amoeba, and it would take a computer now to list their infinite variety. This is quite heartening, for only dead material can be analysed and dissected. Until recently at any rate, Jewish Law with its myriad details has been gloriously alive. Like any living thing, a vegetable, a child, it grows, following no logical principle but its inner spark which has reasons and vitality of its own. Like any other living thing, it is subject to the laws of illness and decay. Neither state comes accidentally, but neither works according to Greek or Roman logic. Both the Lord of Hosts and His people the family of Israel are too passionate for consistency and formalism. From this you will see that the questions the Pharisees put to Jesus were not necessarily trick questions. They were no different from the questions they put to each other. (And which their remaining followers put to each other to this very day.)

The Gospels, too, take this form because they describe the life of a Jew in a Jewish world. The sacraments are not presented in a formal list, in order of importance, but arise out of the circumstances of a life. The Gospels follow the paths of Jewish experience, they use the symbols of Jewish feeling but give them another dimension, and transform them. And all the characters in the Gospel stories are still recognisable in the remnants of old rabbinic ghettos which still remain. Even in its decay, the Jewish suburb and its life give more understanding of Christian origins than scholars have realised. Paradoxically, it is only since the great destruction of Jewish life that this world, which has a living continuity with the life of Jesus, is being examined at all.

Let us try, then, to break the puzzle. Let us try and see the plan of salvation which these details assume. To do so, history is more helpful than theology. The former is holy, it is 'the generations' of the Bible. The latter is a later importation whose foreign origins are still obvious. The key to the puzzle is in another city and a tragic one, the besieged city of Jerusalem in the year 70 of the common era. The Jews fought the rest of the world and lost, and only Jerusalem is left. The armies of Titus surround it, food is running out, and the tension rises. Some say God will never forsake his city. Many say this even today, but it never carries conviction because Jerusalem has fallen many times before. For others, the only answer is heroic death, a defence to the last man. In this crisis a Pharisaic leader speaks out, the eminent Rabbi Yochanan ben Zakkai, and his advice is 'surrender'. They call him a quisling. There is a text in Leviticus which says, 'These laws are given that a man should live by them'. For him and his party duty pointed to life not death – 'to live by them' – not die for them. Heroic deaths are a pagan luxury. Life, even in humiliation, was the way of service to God. The Torah is not a book of the dead, it is a book for the living. The former it scarcely knows. For Judaism, they are in the realm of God, the situation of the living is more complex.

Yochanan, smuggled out of the besieged city in a coffin by his disciples, came before Titus, who greeted him, a noble defector to Rome. He was offered many things, but he asked for this above all – permission to set up a school in a village called Yavneh – a humble request, which was granted without more ado. The strangeness of this request should have given the Romans pause. Materialists, however, always underrate the force, the humility and the strength of ideas. Stalin was not very different when he said, 'How many divisions has the Pope?' Let us imagine similar circumstances in our own times. Hitler, say, has succeeded in invading Britain in 1941, and resistance has almost collapsed.

In this situation the Archbishop of Canterbury turns traitor, and makes his own peace. His reward? Permission to set up a theological college in Cumberland!

From the little school of Yochanan ben Zakkai, which he founded by the sacrifice of patriotism and pride, came the plan which lasted to our own days, whose interpretations Jews still keep, for no other has replaced them. The notes of the discussions, which took place in Yavneh, and those of the colleges which have succeeded it, form the Talmud. This collection is the atelier, the workshop, out of which all later Judasim was created. This is the monument and the glory of the Pharisees and their disciples. It is a vast, untidy, and rambling work. Thousands of people are quoted in it – some saints, some sinners. It is a jungle of argument and debate, through which the reader has to hew a path, needing devotion and intellect.

Do not go to it to see the final product. That can only be seen in the life based upon the Law, which was lived by the vast majority of Jews until modern times. You can still see that way of life in the Jewish suburb today. The open society has made great inroads into it, but it is still discernible. Even when modern Jews have tried consciously to break with the past, and have abandoned their belief and attachment, they are still not free. They still reflect, even against their will, in their attitudes and reflexes, in the way they think and react, the discussions of Yochanan's school, and his pupils' way to God.

Yochanan, and his followers, turned away from philosophy and theology, repelled by the brute force of the Roman Empire and the seemingly pointless word games of Greece. They turned back to the centre of the Torah itself – to law. About one rabbi of that time it is said that if he had lived in another age he would have been a prophet, but the inspiration of God now flowed through legal channels. Law and inspiration hardly seem the same thing. Yet for Jews Law has been for centuries an exciting thing, and a passionate thing, and what is even harder to conceive a lovable thing, something to enjoy, to delight in, to play with even. When Christianity separated itself from Jewish Law, and turned towards the Roman Empire, it gained a world but lost a great

35

prize. Unconsciously it began to think of Law in Roman terms and Law became grand, imposing, dignified, consistent, but external. It ceased to be a delight for the ordinary man, a game he could play, an act of love he could demonstrate. Now Jewish Law is in many ways stricter than any secular law can ever be, but it was kept for millennia, without a police force, or prison system. True there were judges and courts but they had little power in the ages of suppression and persecution. The Law was kept because it inspired love. Law and love are not contradictory terms for Jews for the Law was given in love. That is why people have given their lives and riches for it, because they could not live without it. 'Its ways are ways of beauty', says the liturgy, and 'all its paths are paths of peace.'

What does the Law mean to a Jew? The language he uses to describe it can be ecstatic, like the litanies of the Christian church invoking Mary, the saints, and the Holy Spirit. It turned a rabble into a people. It gave this small people greatness. Through it they alone survive out of all the peoples of the ancient world. Because of it they have never lapsed into barbarism, even when civilisation itself collapsed. Through its discipline, it gives them purity. It takes a businessman, and turns him into a saint. It takes simple people, and gives them grandeur. It takes the ordinariness of a suburb, and makes it a prototype of the Kingdom of God. The dignity and worth of a Jewish suburb do not come from its aesthetic beauty, for it has little, nor from any external grandeur. These are the glories of the pagan world, and Jews are neither Greeks nor Romans.

It is a truism that things are appreciated only by the deprived. Therefore Law has a special importance for Jews, because for so long they have had to live without it. Of course, law courts have always existed in every society. Schools of law flourished in Nazi Germany, and there must be tribunals in the labour camps of the Soviet Union. The power structure of Law is there, but the essence of Law is not. Through the years, Jews have kept the Law, because of its essence, not because of its external power. This seeming powerlessness in fact obliterated the difference between the external and internal demands of God. What had started out written on stone, and had then been transferred to books, had conquered the mind, and had finally been written on the hearts of the Jewish people. It had survived disaster and persecution. In the ordinary Jewish suburbs clustering round modern cities a great drama is being played out, which will affect Jews, and through them all mankind. Can the Law of God survive the compromises of prosperity? Modern life forces people to live on the edge of themselves; their minds concentrated on the rim of their beings. It discourages any journey inwards. The process of Law is reversing, and a deep externalisation has taken place in Jewish life.

In times of prosperity, people become self-reliant – or rather reliant on that part of themselves which takes the least trouble, which requires the least perception. What is outside the senses ceases to be credible, because it is non-sensed, and slips into mere 'nonsense'. Inside Judaism there is a battle, a test – to see if God's will can be done in prosperity as well as in hard times. This struggle inside a Jewish suburb is important, because it is a key to the 'progress' of the surrounding world. Can real generosity and awareness flourish in success? Some positions have already been given up, and God is being nuanced out of the religious exercise. Prayers are said in doubt and addressed 'to whom it may concern'. As this happens nothing seems to change, but everything is transformed. Synagogues become country clubs, rabbis become communal executives (in nice grey charcoal suits and with-it ties). Discussions on Jewish purpose are replaced by rhetorical speeches for Jewish survival. A deep change takes place in Jewish thinking, as the element of holiness is first left out, and then ceases to be understood. God ceases to choose His people, now they can only choose themselves. With this their uniqueness goes, and they become the tailpiece of nineteenth-century nationalism, the last followers of Garibaldi left alive. And the messianic kingdom loses its dimension of awareness and contemplation. The righteous may still sit feasting, with crowns on their heads, but they are no longer gazing at the face of God. The feast has become a rather ordinary party. As unlike other parties, it may be eternal, it is likely to be very tedious.

Does it matter if this battle is lost? It involves more than a crisis in a suburb but also a crisis in the soul of Judaism. We Jews have seriously tried to find God in prosperity and peace. We have worked for His Kingdom, through all the small details of practice and administration. We have done the homework He has set us. We have paid great attention to the little things of life, and tried to do His will on committees. We have not tried to turn the world upside down for religious purposes, letting paradox replace the common sense of Torah and Talmud. But if it is shown that God can only be found in disaster, when men are stretched out of their nature, and purpose can only be found in concentration camps, then we have come to the end of a road. We would then have to replace the symbols of hope and prosperity with those of suffering, and say that men cannot come to their Father without them. This would be the end of Pharisaic Judaism, no matter what scraps of culture remain; it could only turn towards a Christianity without Christ.

For Jews, therefore, the sanctification of a suburb is of enormous importance. It is crucial to the Jewish experiment, joining the world of the spirit with the world as it is, and not with a dream of the world as it should be. For the rabbis did not seek to change the nature of men, and their desires, but to accept them as they had been created, regulating the righteousness of their actions, and giving their lives the dimension of holiness.

Two pictures are given in the Bible of the messianic kingdom. One is found in the prophecies of Isaiah and Jeremiah. The redeemed city, they say, will be full of parties, of the 'simchos' so beloved to Jews. The noise of parades and wedding processions will fill the streets. People will sit in their gardens, sure of their prosperity, their mortgages, and the terror will have gone, together with the insecurities of our time. This is the world that the Pharisees and their pupils tried to build. This is the vision they worked for. But it is not just a picture of any suburb in a time of prosperity. It is a suburb whose centre is with God, which turns every seventh day to a foretaste of a peace, which goes beyond the boundaries of the political world. Woven into the prosperity will be the imprint of God's presence, the wigs, the kosher signs, the time-switches (which avoid making sparks on the Sabbath), the plaited bread, all the strange signposts that point to another land.

Unfortunately there is another picture. It is found in the prophet Amos, and this is the fear of the suburbs. Will the knowledge of God come in a day of darkness and not one of light? Can Jews only be faithful when they are in trouble? These thoughts turn Jews to strange paths, the twilight of the Kabbalah, the attraction of Christianity. These are grandiose thoughts, but for the Pharisees the grandiose was profoundly pagan. The Lord of Hosts had so much magnificence that He did not require the grandeur of human tragedy to accomplish His plan. He was great enough to take up residence in undistinguished suburbs, and legislate for grocery shops – provided, of course, they had kosher labels!

Chapter Four

Holiness at the Kitchen Sink –
the Jewish Home

Enter in peace you servants of peace, messengers of the Most High, of the
King above the kings of kings, the Holy One, blessed be He.

Sabbath Hymn for the Home

Rabbi Jose ben Judah said: The angels of the service accompany a man on
Friday evening from the Synagogue to his house, one good and one bad
angel; and if, when he comes to his house, the lamp is lit, and the table
spread, and the couch arranged, the good angel says: 'May it be God's will
that the next Sabbath may be as this one', to which the bad angel, even
against his will, says: 'Amen'. But if it is not so, then the bad angel says:
'May it be God's will that thus it may be on the next Sabbath also', and the
good angel, against his will, says: 'Amen'.

Talmud Shabbat

When Christians first approach Judaism, they become increas-
ingly puzzled not by what is there, but by what is missing. At the
centre there is a hole, and it is just where the Temple should be.
The priests and the sacrifices have gone. There are no holocausts,
no sacraments, and no mystery. Catholics feel this even more than
Protestants. They recognise an organic connection with traditional Judaism, but in the centre Judaism seems to be as bare
as the most austere Protestant sect. Where has it all gone?

I suggest that they are looking in the wrong place. Jewish
history has not made for triumphalism, but for humility. It is
easier to find what they expect in Canterbury or at St. Peter's in
Rome. There are processions, there is the meeting point of the
faithful, and the administration of a scattered religious world.

There, too, high priests are in residence, and the ecclesiastics and administrators are the modern counterparts of the Cohens and Levys of the Pentateuch. The parallelism, the similarity in the mixture of business and mystery, is not hard to see. Jews hanker, of course, for the same things, and the 'Hechal Shlomo' in Jerusalem is a kind of Vatican. One hesitates to say a poor man's version, it is better to say a scaled-down one. It is significant that it was built in a time of self-confidence after the early triumphs of the Israeli state.

But if Christians and Jews detach themselves from their own pride and triumphalism, they remember that the prophets, the Pharisees, and Jesus as well, stood apart from this external greatness. (It is no accident that all the bad kings of Israel were great builders, but the good ones didn't leave very much behind.) Because they were detached, both Nazarenes and Pharisees were able to build the foundations of new things, after the old shell collapsed. The birthplace of the Christian mystery was not the Temple, but a room on the upper floor of a lodging house in Jerusalem. The things that Jesus saw and touched that evening he could find today in a traditional Jewish home. The great Temple ended. Part of its inheritance, combining oddly with the Latin culture of Rome, entered into the Christian church. In Judaism the inheritance came to rest in the privacy of the home.

The entry of this refugee, this fallen greatness, transfigured the nature of the house, and its occupants. The father became a priest, the mother a priestess, and the dining-room table an altar. The furniture of the Temple from the Holy of Holies itself came to rest beside the salt cellar, the mustard pot and the sauce bottle. The candles, the clothes, the white of the tablecloth brought the holiness and mystery of tremendous events into the surroundings of daily life. In the world of rabbinic Judaism, the synagogue emphasised doing and knowing, but the home was concerned with being, with memory, and experience.

Because of the new Occupier, the Jewish home became a meeting place for both natural and supernatural beings. This hospitality affected Jewish cooking, which does not centre around the steaks and roasts of today, but inclines to casseroles and stews, which are infinitely stretchable. 'Let all who are hungry, come and eat!' says the celebrant at the passover meal in the home. In the Mass or the Eucharist ceremony there are similar words of invitation to a spiritual meal. Among Jews the meal is on a different level of reality, but the same generosity and unselfishness is there. The home has traditionally been open to all God's friends, wherever they live. These are the poor, the widowed, the orphan, the refugee, and the stranger, all of whom are specially mentioned time and again in the five books of Moses. And with them come other beings of God's acquaintance, the creatures who inhabit, so to speak, the interstellar space and the spheres which lie between us and the divine.

Traces of the invisible Guest are everywhere, signs of His marriage to the household of Israel. Passages from Deuteronomy rest in little metal boxes on the doorposts, and the pious kiss or touch them as they enter (in dwindling numbers now). In the cupboards among the glasses and decanters are the candlesticks for the Sabbath lights and a cup for the wine that is blessed, and lying among the napkins is the cloth for the Sabbath bread which will be sanctified. In the cupboards holy and secular meet and jostle, there is no strain, for all things can be transformed if they are turned to God. Cocktail cabinets and the kitchen drawer are the sacristy for the liturgy of the home.

And the changes of the liturgical year are marked out for the Jew by smell and taste, by the aromas of the kitchen. Through the most basic senses, he feels the changing moods of the spirit. Theologies alter and beliefs may die, but smells always remain in his memory, calling him back to his own childhood and to the childhood of his people. Whatever prayers he may forget, the gastronomic cycle always remains. Passover is the bread of poverty, with tears of salt water, and the horseradish of bitterness. Ruth is cream and cheesecake, and the New Year is the sweetness of apples and honey. Esther comes with poppy seed, and the Maccabees with nuts. The delightful litany only halts to mark the destruction of the past, or days which commemorate the sins of the present. On these tragic and sad days there is a total fast, and the kitchen, the heart and soul of the Jewish home, misses a beat, and a darkness covers this little world.

Interwoven into all this joy are the darker threads, reminding the inhabitants that houses do not last for ever, and that the end of the journey is an eternal home, not a co-op in a suburb. The unplastered wall indicates that here is no abiding city, and that Jews are still a wandering people, like Abraham their forefather. It is true we no longer journey through deserts, from oasis to oasis, but from one great city to another. We are still God's wanderers, despite all our sophistication, the Hebrews, the 'ovrim', which some have explained as the people who pass by. This disconcerting blend of experience makes us put a drop of sorrow in all our religious happiness. There is always a bitter sweet taste to Jewish experience.

As the marriage service is about to end and all prepare to go, the bridegroom stamps on a glass and breaks it. He reminds himself of sad things, that love is hard to fashion and easy to break. We raise a cup of wine at the Passover meal and prepare to drink it, remembering the deliverance from the concentration camp of Egypt. Yet we pause, and remove ten drops to remind ourselves of the Egyptian suffering during the plagues. At harvest time, a booth is made in the garden. It is beautiful with flowers and fruit, but according to the Law it must always have a hole in the top, and so be open to the wind and rain. It is not only a memorial to the harvest, and the creator's bounty, but also to man's meanness. It also reminds us of refugee huts, like the ones that were built during the forty years of wandering in the desert, and which were inhabited after each great war in our time.

So the history of the Jewish people becomes part of the Jew, absorbed into his digestion, and his memory. It is not a theology, but an experience, which binds him to a long past, a taste left in the mouth, a smell still hovering about his nose. At the synagogue, he seeks to know God with his mind, but in the intimacy of his home, God joins his family, and effortlessly His presence fills the room, as naturally as the smells and tastes of the religious symbols. And with Him come other visitors, who inhabit the vast distances which separate God and man. Some visit the synagogue too, but most prefer the home, for they were not born from textbooks, like the Golem, the artificial man, of Rabbi Loeb. Rather they were born from the living experiences of people who saw them, so to speak, and felt their presence.

When the Sabbath comes, all the inhabitants, both natural and supernatural, meet together, to celebrate the creation, the birthday of the world. They meet together, united in a kind of birthday party, with candle-light, wine and bread. As with all intimate things, the customs vary from home to home. In some synagogues the company turn to the door as the Bride of the Sabbath enters. She accompanies them to their homes, bringing everyone a gift – a special soul for this day. (The old ones have got rather shabby during the working week.) With her come the ministering angels, the messengers of peace, who wheel into the crowded room with their blessings. And there are stranger figures yet. Elijah, the stormiest of prophets, turns up at the close of the Sabbath, transformed into the comforter, bringing the good tidings of redemption still to come, and the perfect Sabbath that will be. The home has become a lived-in Temple, and the inhabitants are no longer the same, nor their relationships with each other. An other worldly light plays around some very worldly people – it gives them haloes they would not otherwise possess. The father, who may be a tailor or travelling salesman during the rest of the week, now reveals another nature. With covered head and white shirt, raising the beaker of wine in sanctification, he is the priest who purifies the household, whose task is to purify the world. The language seems exalted but it is accurate enough. He is, after all, a member of God's chosen people, 'a kingdom of priests and a holy nation'. This is not just megalomania, nor religious fancy dress, but reasonably accurate theology.

On Friday night this priestly figure turns to an ordinary suburban housewife and addresses her. He compliments her in the words of the Book of Proverbs. She is, he says, a woman of valour, and her price is beyond rubies. The elders praise her in the gates, as do her own good deeds. The high manner and style may seem bizarre to the outsider, invited into the family circle;

45

they are not to Jews who have grown accustomed to joining the smallness of their lives with an extraordinary force, which can exalt the lowly and bring down the mighty. An ordinary hen-pecked husband has become a patriarch without self-consciousness. Before the meal he encircles the children with his hands. The boys are blessed like Ephraim and Menasseh, the girls like Sarah, Rebecca, Rachel and Leah. At the end of the meal, the high style continues, sitting oddly with the bourgeois environment. 'My masters, let us bless the Lord . . .', 'With the permission of my masters . . .'. A bridge is thrown across time, to a past so remote that historians can scarcely reach it, but Jews in worship can and do.

So the links are forged in the home, which join the transcendent to ordinary, known and intimate objects of one's life, and one generation to another, to make those powerful links in the chains of Jewish tradition. 'History' is too abstract a word for Hebrew. It knows 'the generations'. At every meal the work of tradition can be seen, the handing on of experience and feeling, as well as words. In later life the words often disappear, for modern sociology is not kind to Judaism, but the experience never does. The supernatural has for a moment at least touched human life, and it cannot be explained away, or shrugged aside.

There is a great sadness in a Jewish home which has no child. Stories are still told, and songs are sung, but there is no one to pass this inheritance to, and a great commandment cannot be fulfilled. A child is petted, made much of, for without him the purpose goes. He is a figure of hope, a renewal, another chance. His eyes may see what our eyes have not seen – the messianic redemption. He is one step nearer to the consummation of things. When 'a child is born unto us', Jews turn towards religion, for it is a messianic event. Even if the parents do not believe, their children might. There is another pulse in the work of redemption.

However He may appear in later life, at the beginning God reveals Himself to the Jewish child in sweetness. He is the honey on the cake a child receives, as he goes to his first Hebrew lesson – so that the Law may be sweet in his mouth. He is the money, which drops from the pages of his first religious book, hinting at other treasures, which lie within. He reveals Himself in the little Sabbath presents, in toys and coloured pencils and sweets. His are the games of hide-and-seek with the unleavened bread, which conclude the liturgy of Passover. He is almost Santa Claus, but not quite. Every Jewish child knows early in his life that God has another face. Around the family table other stories are told, tales of persecution and suffering, which are not from an heroic past, but from a terrifying present. The child barely understands, but he feels the apprehension which moves round the table, and like his elders turns in closer to the warmth of the sheltering tradition, which is his fortress and his protection.

Tradition also gives parties. Whenever God visits the home, or His saving acts are remembered, a party commemorates the occasion. Games mingle with blessings. Smoked salmon and chicken soup lie alongside the bread and wine that have been blessed. Prayers are interspersed with jokes and laughter, and a glow of happiness and warmth transforms the participants. The good things of this world and the next come together, and here, not in the synagogue, is the foretaste of the everlasting Sabbath, the feast prepared for the righteous, and the joys of the kingdom. For a moment in this life a unity is achieved, and for the rest of the week we live on its memory. As the Sabbath fades, a silver box of spices decorated with bells is passed from hand to hand. So in the working days that lie ahead the family will remember the special grace they have received as they call to mind the perfume and the tinkling music.

These parties which look so simple, so unforced, are really works of art. They are rabbinic Judaism in flower. The restrictions and commands of the Law do not exist in their own right, as penances or mortifications, but to give form to experience. The Laws of the Sabbath are infinite in their detail. No machine may be used. On this night the husband should have intercourse with his wife (provided she is not menstruant). Time-switches are permissible. Money must not be touched. Rattles are probably allowed to calm crying children – for this even the greatest rule of the Sabbath can be set aside. Human ingenuity is encouraged, so that people can feel at home, even when God says 'No'.

Special dishes are eaten, which can be cooked in the dying baker's oven over Friday night. Ingenious machines like samovars, lighted before the Sabbath commences, provide endless tea. Even the housewife and *au pair* have a rest at last, with all creation.

For this is the purpose of each law, and each restriction – rest. Every one of them is like a stroke of paint on a canvas. Individually they make no sense. Together they are a work of art. One day in seven, a family in a modern town returns to the rhythm of a day long ago. It returns in spirit to a quieter and more natural world, divorced from newspapers and success, money, strife, and gadgets. In the quiet they can turn from outer peace to a peace within, that is easier to experience than to understand. An ordinary family, caught up by the pressures and vanities of the world, experiences the seventh day with its contemplation and slow rhythms.

The idyll is still there, but for most Jews it is now on the frontiers of memory. The world became too complicated. One enemy ceased to persecute us from outside but another has come into our spirit. The secular world does not threaten our working days. The committees meet, charity funds are raised, and families and communities work hard for each other. The sacrifice of time, money, and activity never ceases, like the offerings to the Lord in ancient times. It is the seventh day which is in danger, there the crisis is felt.

It is not crisis about one little detail or another, it is a crisis about the very nature of the seventh day. What do we work for? To whom do we dedicate our activity? Why were we put here on earth? If these things are not clear then even good works become an opium, and an evasion of the question of life's purpose. We all seem to want rest, but rest is in fact deeply disturbing. Then we can no longer see ourselves reflected in the minds of others, but in our own or God's, and this is not comfortable. Much love is required before people can be still together, and much trust.

Bewildered Jews would like to keep the secular delights of the Sabbath, but forget the religious reasons for them. It is good for the home, they say, and keeps the family together. It stops

48

husbands from straying, and it is more economic. But the Sabbath, and the Jewish home, were never designed to keep husbands from straying, or to prop up declining suburban lives.

In this place at this time the messengers of God, the ministering angels, entered the home. The humdrum was sanctified, and there was a 'happening', a transfiguration. Many Jews would like to invite the human guests, but not the celestial ones. They have a great problem, for in addition to the little presents, so liked by Jews when visiting, the boxes of chocolates, the bottle of wine, they would also like 'atmosphere'. They hanker for the 'old-fashioned, *heimishe* spirit'. But to get these things you need holiness and angels, and the holy spirit, and if they are not believed in, how can they be invited. Would they feel welcome in such a doubting and doubtful atmosphere? What presents would such celestial visitors bring? What taste would such gifts leave behind? (If they exist, of course!)

Chapter Five

The Synagogue, the Holy Town Hall

What are our places of prayer . . . but schools of prudence, courage, temperance and justice, of piety, holiness and virtue?

Philo

Some people think of business when they are at the Synagogue. Is it too much to ask them to think of God when they are at business?

Nachman Kasovir

The first thing you must understand is that a synagogue is not a church, not a good one, nor a defective one either. It is not the best place to have a religious experience, because it is usually too noisy. Nor is the time of the synagogue service the best time to bare one's soul to God – the word 'I' is too strongly discouraged. It offers little inner hush or foretaste of another reality, and in it no mysteries are celebrated. It was the supplement and the rival rather than the successor to the Temple. The most important prayer in the service, the Shema, is not said to the Almighty – it is assumed He knows it – but the congregation say the words at each other. Only very general things are asked and not many of those, but very decisive statements are made. The traditional service also requires considerable verbal agility on the worshipper's part. Only too often, unable to cope, they drop by the wayside as the long 'order of service' goes remorselessly on, catching up repeatedly how and when they can. The piety is not in the place, but in the people. Samuel Pepys wandered into one once, and was so shocked by the lack of decorum, and the unspiritual behaviour of the 'devout' that he decided never to go again (he chose the most ebullient day in the Jewish calendar – the Rejoicing of the Law).

Synagogues are open to all, and it is best to visit one for oneself. Go in, and look it over carefully. Mentally disregard the ornaments and you will see that it is only a room with a bookcase at the end. In the bookcase – usually a cupboard – there is a scroll containing the five books of Moses. Over the cupboard is a light, a reminder of the presence of God, though as this is self-evident, it is not absolutely necessary for prayer. Sometimes the cupboard is on the dais to symbolise Mount Sinai. Even this dais is a luxury and not essential, for the mountain itself, like the grave of Moses, is unknown and the anonymity intentional. The events there were too poignant and overwhelming for pious tourism. This is a deep Jewish feeling which probably the apostles shared. They didn't, after all, make a Lourdes or Fatima out of Gethsemane. It can be a temporary home for refugees, or a soup kitchen for the poor, and committee meetings can be held in it. It is more than a house of prayer, it is the town hall, the parliament, the meeting hall, and, above all, the university of the community who use it – their holy school. It does not tolerate or know any division of reality.

It is not a phenomenon of the countryside. It has always existed in the heart of towns, surrounded by workshops and tenements. It harbours no dreams for a green and pleasant never-never land. Such trite landscapes are usually found in the vicinity of crematoria. Synagogues are too busy to be tasteful. They are more influenced by the needs of living bad taste than by the landscaped vistas which surround cemeteries and express the good taste of the respected dead.

No one knows how it was born, the strangest and simplest of all places of worship. It arose from poverty during the exile of defeat, after the destruction of all that remained of the great Temple of Solomon. The first synagogues were not opened with pomp and ceremony in Jerusalem, but in obscurity, perhaps in a suburb of an enemy capital, in Babylon or its neighbouring towns. A group of exiles came together, they hired a room to shelter themselves and others, to consider what had gone before, and to argue out of the tradition what God required of them in an alien environment; what laws could still be kept, and what songs of Zion could still be sung on foreign soil. Like all of us they needed a religious home, though they had probably begun to realise that home was not an address but a force which flowed through them, both in their success and in their failure. Home was a power which could destroy the Temple in its strength, and make a hired room the strongest institution of their history. In the synagogue, the objective power of this 'force' and this 'will' is studied. The force itself requires no synagogues, for in the words of the service 'and after everything shall end, alone in wonder will He reign', and again 'As once He was so is He now, the glory that will never change'. It is the devotees, the instruments of the force, who need it. But the synagogue is not even there for their subjective experience, but rather for the upkeep of the world in which they live.

As you enter the synagogue, the noise of prayer and chatter greet you. A conversation between neighbours mingles with the murmuring of a swaying worshipper. The rabbi is reading silently on the dais, two officers of the congregation are beside him, discussing the details of the service. There is a steady flow of people in and out. There is smothered laughter from a Yiddish joke. The atmosphere is disconcerting. The spirit of the outside world surges into the holy place, and it does not seem to be a very holy place at all.

What are the real holy places of a man's life? Where do his deepest experiences occur? Is it in a 'place of worship', or in his place of business? Where does he ask the great religious questions? Perhaps it is when he lies awake on his bed. The psalms certainly indicate this. Perhaps it is in the cafés; some like Leah Goldberg, the Israeli poetess, see God in the smoke of cigarettes. If one is going to make hierarchies of holy places, Jewish feeling would probably choose the home – for there the joy of holiness is most concentrated and most felt.

The synagogue then is not the highest or the holiest, but it is certainly the busiest centre of a man's life in religion, and it assumes that there is no life that is not in religion. God is present in one's life and in the world. A synagogue, a holy place, does not make Him present – it helps the worshipper or the student (there is little distinction between the two among Jews) to recognise it as being there. God's will is accomplished whether with or without our consent, says the Talmud. Study and prayer help us to be conscious of it.

The confused noise of the synagogue has its own greatness. It testifies to a holy unity of what goes on outside with what goes on inside. Chatter in the synagogue assumes prayer in the market place. Just as material preoccupations surge into the building, so the knowledge of God surges out into the details of daily life. A man eats, sleeps, makes love, and prays. All are necessary for the world in which he has been placed, and of which he is an integral part.

Because of what it is the synagogue tells us that religion is functional and necessary to our lives. It is not an ornament, no matter how beautiful, and the synagogue experience is certainly not an aesthetic one. It has more in common with the clothes we wear, the medicines we take, than with the art pictures on the wall. The former are essential to us, the latter are luxuries, the cherries on the cake. It is nice to have religion with good taste, but this is not always granted. Ghettos and concentration camps have no aesthetic merit, though the world can live for many years on their religious merit.

The refinements of the synagogue, though occasionally beautiful, have a haphazard appearance. Jews have passed through too many cultures, and passed through them too quickly at that, to imbibe much feeling for classical unity and purity of form. Unlike the ancient Greeks, such things were nice enough, but definitely not top priority. If the building is old (fifty years by Jewish standards, such is the insecurity of Jewish life) then the architecture will marry elements of Poland, Russia, Islamic Spain and the German middle ages in one building. If it is modern, the result will usually be suburban good taste, in the style of London and New York. Since Jews have taken to modern art, there will also be some modified Bauhaus. The rabbi's gown will be

'Geneva' cut, and his hat Russian Orthodox with or without Catholic pompoms. The verger might be top-hatted in the Victorian manner and his gown modified Anglican. The music, which is probably the most beautiful element aesthetically, will usually be based on Mendelssohn with occasional rhythms from Eastern Europe, enriched by tones from the Orient, Israeli folk music, and in England genteel reminiscences of the palm court orchestra. The general effect is that of a lived-in home, in which a family has collected some intrinsically lovely things and mementoes, sometimes sentimental, sometimes moving, of its life experience. It is this sense of life which prevents the ensemble from absurdity. Even in its attempt at grandeur, the synagogue points to the hired room which was its origin.

Decoration and grandeur are impermanent things. Wealth and security can be enjoyed but cannot be held. Jews are a wandering people, not because of their own inclinations, but because of their religious history. Any group which journeys, which goes on a pilgrimage, be it a person or a church, may enjoy but must not get too attached to the landscape through which it passes. Attachments can be formed to a style of service, to a culture in which one has settled, to patterns of religious leadership, to clothes, to beautiful things, and even to well-loved absurdities. Just because they do not last for ever, such things are not bad, as much 'spiritual' thinking implies. After all, we share the same finiteness. Nor are passing things necessarily tragic as the Greeks considered. The end of the journey does not invalidate the experience on the way.

The synagogue proper today is usually a praying area, at the centre of a complex of rooms, and a rabbit warren of huts and prefabs. No matter how carefully the Jewish authorities plan, Jewish history always disconcerts them. They plan for something static and the Jewish world is always on the move. Great buildings, erected in living memory, become empty shells, and London is littered with dying synagogues. Their plaques are dotted through Europe as well. In any city of Spain, Poland or Germany there is always a tiny remnant of an old synogogue which time has bypassed. To compensate for this, other synagogues grow up like Topsy, to accommodate the new refugees. For such a people, a tent might be more suitable, or the moving tabernacle of the exodus.

Consider these additions carefully, for they are not optional extras, bits to be hidden behind a stately and pretentious façade. They are integral parts of the synagogue itself. For the synagogue is not the Temple of Jewish life, the holy of holies, but it is the religious town hall, where the will of God is not only discovered in prayer and argument, but where it is also implemented. The committee rooms, the offices, the filing cabinets are the logical result of the praying areas. Together they form a unified work. In a good synagogue both spill over into each other. A bunch of men say memorial prayers in a room while an animated discussion about communal behaviour takes place before the Ark. The connection between being and doing is very close, and in Jewish history the latter usually comes first.

In the desert the children of Israel exclaimed 'Let us do it, and then hear it'. This is the order of Jewish priorities to this day. There is not much point in finding out the will of God if it is not going to be translated into action. Such knowledge becomes indeed positively harmful. If it is never exposed to reality, it is best that it remains in the dark. Dead knowledge only grows flaccid with non-use and develops gangrene. A great deal of Jewish law today is no longer observed. It no longer produces action, only guilt. It has the diseases of decay.

A synagogue is a religious machine which is always trying to turn prayers into deeds. As the service ends, people form little clusters, and only the fear of a burnt meal and the pangs of hunger drive them away from the synagogue steps and from the informal little committees the prayers have inspired. The chatter and the debate at the door are holy, because through them the word of God is preparing to act in the world. The words, the buzz of conversation, are the intermediaries, the messengers who cross the abyss which divides God from His creation, bringing the will of eternity to the needs of the human beings who live next door.

Neighbours usually deplore the noisiness of synagogues.

Prayers, chatter and argument form a unity in Jewish religious life. The mixture is efficient, though not relaxing. 'The Holy One, blessed be He, neither slumbers nor sleeps', says the Prayer Book. He is at work, but what is His job, what does He work at? The rabbinic answer is simple : the same things that we work at. Only He does it without reward, and for no ulterior motive. He dowers the brides, visits the sick and accompanies the funeral processions where there is no other mourner.

Jews give more charity per head than any other group of people. They do so because it is an integral part of their Opus Dei – of their liturgy. The Torah, which is written on the scroll like other holy writings, is kissed, but as it is a book it is more important to read it, and more important than reading it, is doing it. The prayers in the synagogue drive worshippers into the world, they do not hold them back in meditation. Old-age homes, money for Israel, ambulances, aid to refugees, pour out from the Jewish liturgy. They are the sacrifices of thanksgiving of the people, and also their sin-offerings. Enormous attention is given to the upkeep of society, and people's responsibilities to each other. Jews argue about the niceties of liturgy as a kind of luxury – a God-permitted sport. They become more serious when they get down to the work of tombolas, and raffles, and fund-raising. Occasionally, in the refined religiosity of the upper middle class, rabbis today suffer from a confusion of roles. 'Is all this just a little sordid?' they wonder. 'Is it not just a little vulgar?' 'Is it right to think so much about the daily bread of life and its cost?' This is in fact exactly what the Torah writes about, among other things, of course.

'You shall love the Lord your God, with all your heart, and with all your soul, and with all your might', says the great Jewish prayer which comes from Moses himself. Heart and soul, oddly enough, presented little problem to the commentators. They had more difficulties with the word 'might'. One interpretation was that it meant all one's bodily strength. The interpretation that hit home, however, and which was implemented in daily Jewish life, was that it meant 'money', i.e. that we should love God with all our money and our wealth. Such is the holy materialism of Judaism. Our ancestors brought sheep and goats and bullocks to God, because these were their money, the hard currency of those times. We bring our earnings too. Is there anything better? Do words, or thoughts, or dreams have more value?

Before the last war in London, Jewish women at dead of night used to go round the blocks in the poor parts of Jewish London, dropping money in the letter boxes, so that every poor family might have some joy and security on the Sabbath or Festivals. This was a very high type of giving, when no one's feelings were hurt, and God alone knew who gave and who received. The giving is more obvious now, for giving has become a science and an industry – it always was an art! Moreover, the persecutions, and Israel demanded prodigies of giving from a very small people. The methods are more showy now, because more has to be raised, the essential thing, however, is that it is given. This is our minimum service to God in the world. It is the completion of the liturgy – the 'amen' at the end.

Jews are usually so concerned with details and with the present that they rarely ask themselves about the institution to which they give so much in time, energy and affection. They question its existence and purpose as little as they question the existence and purpose of their home. Both have always been there and in both there is always a place ready for them. They are not given to theology, and therefore do not stop to think what a synagogue is – a holy workshop, the prototype of the Kingdom, and God's town hall and university. Wherever a synagogue exists, the Jewish experiment is in progress, for the religion of the Pharisees is not a protest or an opposition, it is a continuous attempt to construct a society which is a reflection on earth of what is above. It takes words seriously, like an engineer or scientist, especially such words as 'Thy will be done!'.

Such a strong link exists between the synagogue and the society around it, that the sickness of one infects the other, there is so little division between them. Formerly the tides of religious awareness flowed from the synagogue into the daily life of the community. There was no artificial barrier between them. Today the tides of secularism flow from the outside world back into the synagogue. Once again no artificial barrier separates them. Because the outside world has lost its religious character, the synagogue has had to become more consciously religious, perhaps artificially so. There is a great stress now on decorum, and on the sermon. Children no longer play between the pews. The arguments get fewer, and the Jews are more self-conscious. They no longer dispute before the ark, or relax with a volume of Talmud, and a glass of lemon tea. God has to be treated with respect, because there is a distance between Him and His people. If you don't know someone well, it's better not to take liberties or to be over familiar. Probably the marble halls will have to be given up, together with the organs and the building funds, for He is really a desert God, who revealed Himself in odd places – at a waste place in Sinai, and in hired rooms in Babylon.

Chapter Six

Prayer - the Inner Work

He who is about to pray should learn from a common labourer, who sometimes takes a whole day to prepare for a job. A wood-cutter who spends most
of the day sharpening the saw and only the last hour cutting the wood, has
earned his day's wage.

Mendel of Kotzk

He prays for the sake of his soul as he takes food for the sake of his body.

Judah Halevi

Hebrew is an ingenious language. One small change, the addition
of a syllable, and a word can change its direction. If a certain
syllable is prefixed to a word, the direction and the sense turn
inwards – the action is something done to oneself. The Hebrew
word for prayer has this syllable. A Jew does not pray primarily
to ask for things, nor to have an experience, nor even to feel
God's grace; he prays as he does his other tasks, to do his
duty, to fulfil his obligation, to carry on the work of the world,
and restate the facts and truths of existence with regularity. This
Hebrew word for prayer has little to do with the 'praying' or
'begging' or 'asking' of other traditions. It is not an attempt to
persuade or nag the universe to go off course, for the sake of our
desires. No descendant of the Pharisees would ever confuse
religion and fairy-tales like this. Private prayers are said by Jews
within and without the service. According to one rabbi, prayers
of petition were 'holy impertinence', and 'assaults on heaven'.
Judaism is the wine of its people, it gives them their lift, but it
is not their opium with its fantasy images. The troubles of

Jewish history needed intellect and common sense to face them, and to live with them, but survival has no use for fairy-tales; it forces us instead to truth and realism. Leisured people with comfortable and settled security can afford to shape the truth and play with it. They can retreat into high-bred fantasy. The insecurities of Jewish life, and its precarious comforts, have forced on Jews a healthy respect for what is. 'Truth is our King', says the Prayer Book in every service. Religion is not the construction of the world we should like, but a way to know and accept the reality in which God has placed us.

What, then, is this Hebrew word, whose sense turns inward, and which stands for prayer? Some say its original meaning is 'to work on oneself', others 'to bore a hole in oneself', or 'to judge oneself'. Christians ask God to work in them, so that they can give themselves to Him completely and freely. A Jew prays so that he can work on himself for the sake of God, and shift his own will to become a better instrument of God's will.

The central Jewish prayer is not really a prayer at all, in the conventional sense. It is the recitation of some short extracts from Deuteronomy and Numbers which say few things but say them very forcibly. It states that God is One, with all that follows from it, i.e. that He is alive, unique, all-demanding, infinite, and therefore beyond thought. It also states that one should love this being, rather than respect Him detachedly. He may be an 'It', but one should have the same intensity of feeling and passion for this 'It' as for the closest and dearest of human relationships. Then this 'prayer' enumerates a number of very practical steps that should be taken so as not to forget all this, for what we do has consequences which cannot be wished away, i.e. reward and punishment. Finally, it says that this 'Him' or 'It' is the only reality on which our people can rely in their history. No other force will rescue us from the enemies we make, or release us from the traps we set for ourselves.

These statements, which serve as prayer, are used by a Jew in the same way as a Christian uses the 'Our Father'. He says it morning and evening. It is written on his doorposts, and it is the last thing he says as he dies. It is called the 'Shema' because it opens 'Listen!' or 'Hear!'. This is not said quietly, but loudly. God does not have to be told that he is One – presumably He knows it – but our fellow Jews do. We remind our relatives, the family of Israel, of the reality which governs our destiny. The key Jewish prayer is therefore really not said to God at all, it is said to ourselves, and, above all, we say it at each other. We have publically stated the truth, and fulfilled our duty. We have put the reality of God's Kingdom above all its competitors. This is prayer!

And what, say the rabbis, is the opposite! What is not prayer? – an anti-prayer in fact, and a religious waste of time when there is a lot to do, and time is in short supply. Perhaps, returning after a journey, you see on the horizon the smoke of a fire within the city. You pray spontaneously, 'Lord, may it not be my house!' This is a religious waste of time. It either is your house or it is not. The prayer will not make any difference, and the act of prayer is not meant to. It is realistically speaking a non-starter, and in rabbinic eyes it is a non-prayer.

It takes time to get used to the objectivity and detachment of such prayers. To understand them, remember that work is the key to Judaism, and prayer is only a kind of work. There is the work we have to do in our jobs, there is the work we do in the service, and the work we have to do inside ourselves. They come from the same source requiring the same devotion. There is a lot of work to do for the sake of God's Kingdom. Both the synagogue 'service' and the service of God require a good head, precision and effort. Some Jews want to surrender themselves to God, but for most Jews this is too passive and too feminine to be religiously respectable. (Judaism in its ritual form is patriarchal, though economically it is a matriarchal society.) Years of psychoanalysis are necessary to bring a glimmer of self-awareness or a minute shift in the ego. This indicates the amount of work in prayer that has to be done for real awareness.

If the aim of Judaism is a change in the world, can we bypass the stumbling-blocks in ourselves? The disasters of Jewish history have shown us that this is a pipe-dream – dabblers in politics, please note! We cannot change the world as the Torah commands unless we change ourselves, for we are the world too, and the work begins at home. If we do not see what is inside us, we will always project our inner ignorance on to the world around us, and falsify it consciously or unconsciously with our desires, our hopes, and our fears. We will never have the detachment to see the Truth that is our King, and we won't want to see it either. It is more interesting to change others (for their own good, of course) than to give ourselves an honest look.

The transformation of what exists is the aim of Christians and Jews. But they approach it in different ways. A Christian starts by saving his soul, and ends by saving the world, provided he has not stopped at pietism and forgotten the world, but forged ahead to holiness. The Jew tries to change the world, and finds he has to redeem himself in the process. His progress, too, can be halted, and instead of journeying from righteousness to holiness, he can end up by being side-tracked into politics. This is his own Jewish form of evasion. Good works and ethical theories exist in their own right, they are not substitutes for self-awareness.

Talking about Jewish prayer in the abstract doesn't get you very far, because Jews are not an abstract people. (Biblical Hebrew contains hardly any abstract nouns.) Jews come to God through their feelings, their minds, their successes and their failures. They can't short-circuit them, and they don't really want to.

Go then into a synagogue, and sit down with a Prayer Book. Flick through the pages! The paragraphs do not ask for much, but they make quite a lot of statements, each one rounded off with a blessing. This is what exists, the paragraphs say, this is what you are, these are the realities under which your life is lived and your destiny worked out. Such is the Master whom you serve, and this is what He demands. It assumes that you must bless this reality, though it is not always easy, and sometimes barely possible.

Such a structure seems logical enough, but rather rigid. Yet when these statements are examined an interesting discovery is made. Firstly, they don't seem to agree, and secondly there is occasionally something like deliberate misquotation and pious cheating (if you know enough to see it). Most Hebrew para-

graphs walk in pairs, like animals into the ark, and each paragraph seems to be talking to its fellow. Both are thinking about
the same subject, but they do not hold the same point of view,
and the pious worshipper is caught in the middle. 'Which is
true?' he asks. Both say, 'me'. The answer to a Jewish question
is always another question. Prayer leads us from problem to
problem, but the prayer and the problem mature in the process
and this is religious growth.

The service commences, and the work of prayer begins. One
paragraph asserts that everything we do is worthless, its companion insists on the glory of the good works we can do, and
their value. Another paragraph points to the immensity of the universe, its stunning power, its plans and purposes, which differ so
widely from our own, and to the force and knowledge which lie
beyond it. Yet its companion paragraph turns away from this
transcendence, and this awe to words of rhapsody. How loving,
how tender, is the creator of this vastness, with what love He
feels for us! The language is more startling than a Christian
would at first realise, for 'love' in Hebrew includes not only
'agape', but also 'eros'. ('To know' in Hebrew also includes 'to
love'.) Another paragraph talks about Israel as if it were separate
from the rest of humanity, as if the work of the Children of
Israel, and their destiny were totally apart from the realm of
other human beings, and they were indeed different from other
men. It is answered by its companion paragraph, which points
to a time when all will meet together, and the boundaries of
sympathy, and the frontiers of prejudice will be removed.

The worshipper is thrust into this dialogue. He is pushed into
the dialectic of realism, and between these statements he must
thread his way. God is the union of opposites, and resolution of
them he can never know in his lifetime. Because of our human
condition, reality is always fragmented for us. We are so con-
structed that we can only know by opposites. To surrender to
one or other pole of truth and experience would bring disaster,
and make the work we all must do impossible. Like all other
animals, the Jew needs all his faculties to survive in such immensity, and he needs to believe in himself, and in his aspirations to

journey on. One thing he can not do, he is not permitted to decrease the distance between the opposites. This would be to falsify the world, and religion is reality and not a fairy-story, as I have said, and the creation must be respected as it is.

This dialectic is not a liturgical device or a philosophical fashion, it indicates a reality in the Jewish psyche, and in the ways Jews experience the world. The Prayer Book with its opposing paragraphs is the mirror of Jewish life and a Jew is born into a world of conflicts. These conflicts are very real for him. Throughout his life a Jew will be pulled by the opposite poles of his people's experience. There will be the God, who reveals Himself in the warmth of his home, and the terrible power that has a message for him even in persecution. There is the God who let six million die, and the God who restored a state lost for millennia.

Perhaps it won't be as dramatic as that. Perhaps the worshipper will want to marry a Jewish girl, but fall in love with a gentile one – a small contradiction for the sociologist, but a painful one for him. Behind him there will stretch two cultures, and two streams of memory, and maybe more. He will never be able to feel himself a simple Englishman, or a simple Jew even, or indeed a simple anything. He will look at himself through the many different spectacles that life will force him to wear, and he will know the enlightenment which comes with alienation. The way to God for him is within his own complexity. Like the Jewish worshipper, he must thread his way between the poles of contrasting truth, accepting the complexities of his life, and not longing for the simplicities and comforts which God gave to others.

There are times when this division in the nature of things is transcended in life, and in the liturgy which reflects this life. There is a hymn which is close to the hearts of most Jews, and which has the engaging quality that it can be sung to virtually any tune from Beethoven to Sigmund Romberg. The author is unknown, probably a pious self effacing Spanish Rabbi of the middle ages. In the first lines, the poet speaks of the transcendent God, unknowable, without comparison. We can neither harm Him nor benefit Him. But then, without a break in the lines or the feeling, the poet triumphantly continues with the most commonplace and intimate picture of God. 'God is the flag I wave', he says, 'the cup I drink, the rock I grasp.'

The pious unknown had made the great journey. He had united the known, and what is beyond knowledge, the world of the intellect, and the world of experience. He had brought together the different levels of reality. It is so well done that despite the startling change in ideas, the break is scarcely noticed – there is no seam.

He had done what the painter Vermeer did in another land, in another medium and at another time, in his painting of the city of Delft. It is the real normal city – look, you can see the brickwork! But a stillness and peace have been imparted to it, so subtly that one can not see how it was done, for as in the poem no seam is visible. Two realities have been put together and there has been no cheating and no distortion. The medieval Jewish rabbi and the Dutch painter shared the same experience. Neither simplified the problem, both experienced the problem's inner simplicity and unity.

Jews worship a unity, and they serve it by uniting all their experience. This experience is so varied, and stretches over so many cultures, that it is an emotional necessity for a Jew to do so. The alternative is to accept a permanent schizophrenia. The tortuousness of Jewish argument, and the elaborate commentaries arise because no element of experience or truth can be left out of the equation. God is not served by a false simplicity. His goodness is not preserved for Jews by the existence of a devil. Jews are not kept from sin by division, by polarising the afterlife into heaven and hell, and its inhabitants into sheep and goats. He has to accept the seeming contradictions of the world, and only occasionally does the tradition hold out a helping hand, as he faces the light and darkness which is God.

In the Prayer Book is a sentence, repeated in every morning service. We are asked to bless God 'who forms light and creates darkness, who makes peace and creates all'. This is a deliberate and merciful misquotation of the prophet Isaiah, who could still pray to a God, who was not only 'the maker of peace' but also 'the creator of evil'. We may know this in our hearts, but we cannot say it aloud. Perhaps God was in the gas chambers of Auschwitz, for we know that the day of the Lord may be darkness not light, but if we dwell on it, we may lose our reason, and be incapable of doing our work. The force of reality is so overwhelming that even Jews need some protection against it. Otherwise we too, like poor van Gogh, may cut off our ears. Peace and harmony are desired by all men. Jews are not romantics but realists, and know that they cannot be purchased cheaply.

Christians also have the same problem, as they seek to unify body and spirit, the reality of this world and that of the life to come. They too know the problem which lies at the heart of the unknown Rabbi's poem. The answer for them, however, is different, perhaps easier – the Incarnation joins the two parts. For them the Unknowable has a birth certificate, and people ate, joked and shared a meal with the Infinite. This also seals together the two parts of the poem. But Jews have the harder task. Occasionally we feel God's presence, but His centre is far away, and very different from any man's. Yet we must feel the warmth and intimacy of human love for what can never be 'cosy' or even really knowable. A Jew feels he has to take reality 'neat'. He is not allowed to sentimentalise the transcendent.

Is it necessary to experience God in order to work for Him? For most people the answer is an emphatic yes, especially if the work is prayer. For Jews it is not quite so certain. We were not put into the world to experience His presence. The synagogue service is shaped by the older service of the Temple, and prayers take the place of the old sacrifices. When a man saw the flesh of his animal burning, he saw his capital literally going up in smoke. The forms of sacrifice may be primitive, but their meaning is not – because it is a giving, not a taking. Synagogue prayers which substitute for them have this same characteristic. There is pleasure in religion, but it comes from giving, and the greatest pleasure is giving without strings.

Religious experience is not the payment for prayers. It is important to state this now, for our society is a pleasure-seeking one. It quickly turns from one source of pleasure to another, as it seeks what is beyond pleasure. It favours the quicker and more immediate forms. Sex, drugs and power are all investigated. Therefore it will eventually try the last pleasure of all – the pleasure of mysticism and religious experience. Perhaps even this is not the last pleasure, but only the last but one. The pleasure of final destruction is truly the last. The search may lead to enlightenment, but it may equally well lead to transcendental hedonism and nothing more.

God is not a person, and there always remains a distance between Him and us. We are close, but apart. He loves us, and we are commanded to love Him, but He can never be our pal. We describe this relationship in human terms, but it is not a human relationship at all. Traditionally a Jew makes wedding rings round his fingers in the morning, with the straps of his tephillin. He uses the language of marriage and the language of family relationships (God is the beloved or the father). Yet before all of them he mentally prefaces the words 'as it were'. To prevent undue expectations, the cosiness is constantly dissipated by use of the title 'the King above the king of kings'. Blessings start out by talking to God as 'You', change their standpoint very quickly, and retreat to a safer third person, God can never be 'one of the boys'. Even the majestic names are inadequate, because they are also images, and behind them is the *Ein Sof*, the 'mysterium tremendum', which is beyond all categories of thought. It is scarcely possible to pray to such remoteness, let alone serve it, and give one's life for it. Only very few Jews like Maimonides, who was likened to a cold fire, have ever been capable of such an attachment. Most of us require more colour, more familiarity, and greater reassurance.

Not long ago a semi-humorous consumer guide was produced on religions. It asked 'Which gave most for the least possible investment?' Judaism came out badly – it was low on the list of spiritual choices. Jews are expected to do an awful lot, on awfully little religious experience. Because of this, they can and do feel proud. They are faithful even in hard times, when there is little to comfort them. In fact their response to hard times has always been to increase their obligations. Whatever their faults, and they have many, Jews have never made Judaism a good-time religion, and have never remained in it for what they could get out of it. The cultural confusion of the Jewish world, and the uncertainty of style which results from it, can lead to a vulgarity of manner, but in this they are not vulgar. Observant or not, it does not occur to them to think that God was there to serve them. They have always known it was the other way round.

A crisis has come to the Jewish world. For centuries Jews have found the will of God by meditating on Torah and on Israel, i.e. the laws which have been handed down, and the needs of the people's daily life and existence. Most Jews in our time have abandoned vast stretches of Jewish Law and tradition, and it is unlikely that they will ever return. But what is Israel? As the nightmare of the Nazi past recedes, it becomes more difficult to see Israel's purpose and identity, as the Middle East lurches from one confused crisis to another. There are so many 'Israels' in politics, in religion, and in folklore. Torah and Israel were the old pathways to God, but in our time the way may be reversed. We may have to return to God before we can find our way back to the meaning of Israel and Torah. The past centuries of Jewish life have been marked by study and law. The new conditions may call us to prayer, and the experience of divine things.

There is always a hopefulness about Jewish life, no matter what the crisis or condition, and every Jewish service ends with a note of buoyancy, expressing the irrepressible optimism of the people. Memorial prayers come at the close of the service. The words are startling and very Jewish. 'May His kingdom come in your life-time and in the lifetime of your children!' The dead are with God. Although this prayer is one said for them, it is typical that it does not mention them. For the dead, human prayer is not their greatest need. It is their children, the next generation, who need them.

As Jews think of their own lives, and the persecutions they have known, their sincerest prayers are for the human future. This is something for which prayers are necessary, this is some-thing they can shape. Whether it is Passover in the home, or the prayers in the synagogue, all Jewish services end by turning to the future – the day when God's kingdom will be established not only in the hearts of a believer here, or a believer there, but solidly on earth, directing the nations, and their societies. Paul spoke of three virtues – faith, hope and charity. These are also Jewish ones too, but Jews incline temperamentally to the second. They prayed about hope in the Warsaw Ghetto, and cracked jokes while wearing the Star of David. The national anthem of Israel is called 'The Hope'. This is the unworldly worldliness of their prayers, which state so much and ask so little.

Chapter Seven

How Odd of God . . .

Question: How odd of God,
to choose the Jews!
Answer 1. Oh no it's not,
God knows what's what!
Answer 2. But not so odd
as those that choose,
a Jewish God,
and spurn the Jews.

What makes God happy? To see a poor devil who finds a treasure and returns it.

Yiddish proverb

The vast majority of Jews never chose to be Jews, they were born into it. They did not choose God, God chose them, and there is not much they can do about it, even if they wanted to. This sense of destiny, of predestination almost, has been intensified by recent persecutions. In the middle ages, baptism was a passport to freedom. The wonder is that so few people used it! There was no ceremony, however, which could change the blood in one's veins, or blot out one's ancestors. There was no act or confession which could take Jews off the train to the concentration camp. 'A Yid I was born, and a Yid I am,' goes a folksong. This trite statement was good theology and painful reality.

For Jews, then, the major fact of their life has been decided without their having been consulted. Perhaps this is true for everybody, but for Jews it is conscious and obvious. This realisation goes back very far into the Jewish past. It is stated quite brutally in the early Talmud. 'Without your consent you are born and without your consent you live and without your consent you die, and without your consent you will have to give an account and a reckoning before the King above the King of Kings, the Holy One, blessed be He.'

Jewish problems therefore do not centre on conversion, or conversion experience. That stage has been passed, whether we like it or not. By being born, we find ourselves on a moving train, God is the driver, and it is not easy to get off. 'Spirituality' for a Jew is his response to this situation, not his choice of it. This fact, this objectivity, makes us wear our spirituality (and its problems) with a difference. From the outset we are conscious of another will, greater than our own, whose power modifies our lives and our plans. Religion is not our subjective experience, to be cultivated in order to be visible, but an objective fact. It is not something sought in the recesses of the human heart, it is only too clear in daily experience.

Jews, then, are normal people who got caught up in God's plan of salvation by a whirlwind. They have to live their lives as best they can, sandwiched between the force of the spirit and the resistance of the world. The journey has its thrilling moments, but the ride is neither comfortable nor cosy.

Being very ordinary, most Jews have no wish to be great saints, great sufferers or indeed great anything. They have no wish to live on the edge of madness or inspiration and they turn to their religion to help them live ordinary lives in an extra-ordinary situation. Religion is not there to intensify the emotions, it is there to make them usable and livable with day by day. Anti-semitism, prejudice, refugees, states of emergency, and persecution are not experiences of a moment, they are facts to be lived with, all one's life. The synagogue, the Law and the myriad details of Jewish custom are not there to provide an extraordinary experience, they are there to stabilise it, analyse it and cut it down to size. The chosen-ness and peculiarity of Jewish history are odd enough in themselves, they need no underlining.

Spirituality means something different to a Christian and to a Jew because they live in different situations. God has set them different tasks, and they have different needs. For Christians, spirituality is a push upwards or a way inwards – an adventure of the soul, which journeys out into a dark night. For a Jew spirituality is a way to be normal in the night of persecution and the darkness of continuous insecurity. For a Christian, Jewish spirituality is always pedestrian. For a Jew, the Christian's path is fantastic. Hurts come when people misunderstand each other because they are close, not when people are distant and never understand each other at all.

One of the great tasks of Jewish spirituality is accommodating oneself to the will of God and remaining upright in the process. Since this is very different from the tasks of other traditions of spirituality, it has to use very different means. The most typical weapon of Jewish spirituality is humour. This is in short supply in most scriptures. There are puns and word games in the Old Testament as well as in the New, and probably far more irony than we realise. There is a kind of laughter in the story of Joseph, and God surely has His tongue in His cheek in the last conversation with Jonah outside the walls of Nineveh. Yet the fact remains that there are not many real jokes in either. God and His people register anger and joy, but they do not grin very often.

Humour is a late-comer to Jewish life. The first real jokes which an ordinary man, who is not a scholar, can really laugh about occur in the Talmud. Until then most of the writings are as humourless as those of Karl Marx (both are moral, powerful, sarcastic and not very funny, though the Bible is more open). Humour wells up in the Jewish people as the Temple goes down, together with the recognisable landmarks of Jewish life. Both Christianity and Judaism had to cope with a worldly defeat. The former uses paradox and turns a worldly defeat into a victory of the spirit. The latter tries to live with defeat, as a normal condition of existence, and uses humour to do so. Almost surreptitiously, like a thief in the night, God's oddest and most healing gift stole into the hearts of His people, changing the dourness of their character. So the descendants of the stiff-necked Hebrews end up by doing His will on the New York and London

75

stage or in a Hollywood film, changing bitterness into laughter and purging failure and depression.

The old revelations were in Hebrew. The Word which came to the Prophets was clothed in the stateliness and power of that desert language. The dancing quality of the new gift needed another medium. Unheralded by trumpets, despised by scholars, jargons emerged among the Jews to express this unexpected unlooked-for grace. Alongside the Hebrew Don Quixote, grandly out of step with the world, ride some Sancho Panza figures – Yiddish with its jokes, and Ladino with its love songs. Only now when both are almost dead, killed by the humourlessness and hate of the Nazis, are they appreciated and known for what they are. The world turns to these jokes for their compassion, their insight and their power.

This humour of the Jews is not merely light relief, it is extremely profound. It takes the bitterness of the human heart, and reduces kings, emperors, and dictators, down to size. Groucho Marx also 'removes the mighty from their thrones, and exalts the humble'. The same inversion is experienced in his old jerky films as in the *Magnificat* of Mary. In Jewish jokes Hitler is not a hated figure but a pathetic one. The joke, the 'witz', is the vehicle of compassion. It is in humour that God comes close to the Jews, and through them to all men. Bud Flanagan, the Marx brothers, Danny Kaye, and the countless comedians of Jewish life (every family has one) are the therapeutae who bring healing to the wounded spirits of men.

Today spirituality is an industry, not an art. It has its text-books and degrees. People lecture in it, and their students major in it. We try to make everything neat and respectable, even inspiration itself. God, however, has other ideas, and His choice (not ours) of vessels and messengers never lacks surprise. He has, so to speak, a catholic taste. In times past God spoke through patriarchs and prophets. Later His inspiration came through lawyers and rabbis, as His people tried to reshape their lives after disaster. Today living channels of His word are even more various – writers, comedians, or a teenager in Amsterdam. His message has made them extraordinary. Out of the disasters in Jewish history have come great religious works, which have interpreted them to a bewildered people. Nothing like this has arisen out of the last holocaust. Or perhaps it has, but we have been too snobbish to notice, the divine consolation in the Jewish jokes of the period, and in the *Diary of Anne Frank*. And this unexpected zany revelation has crossed the frontiers of the Jewish world, and entered the world of the Christian spirit. Alongside the staid catholic archangels of the Polish writer Zbigniew Herbert, there is another with a Yiddish name, who sneaks across the frontiers of heaven and hell with the humour, that God gave to the Jews in their distress.

The seventh angel
is completely different
even his name is different
Szemkel . . .

Szemkel
is black and nervous
and has been fined many times for
illegal import of sinners . . .

between the abyss
and the heavens
without a rest his feet go pit-a-pat

Szemkel Szemkel
. . . the angels complain
why can't you be splendid?

the Byzantine artists
when they paint all seven
reproduce Szemkel
just like the rest

because they fear
they might lapse into heresy
if they were to portray him
just as he is
black nervous
with his halo tarnished.

Humour is not just an alleviation of pain, it also brings the infinite down to earth. God has no human form in Jewish theology but He reveals a very human psyche in Jewish jokes. There He enters into the suffering and paradoxes of the world, and experiences the human condition. There He is immanent, if not incarnate, and a gossamer bridge of laughter stretches over the void, linking creatures of flesh and blood to the endlessness of the *Ein Sof*, and the paralysing power of the Lord of Hosts.

Humour is the great solvent which counteracts the rigidity to which Judaism is prone. When a religion concentrates on community and external acts as Judaism does, it is subject to definite diseases. It is so concerned with doing, as opposed to being, that its assessment of spirituality becomes mathematical. Jews tend to tot up the number of commandments they have kept, and then look at everybody else's totals and compare results. In this pietistic game the one with the highest number wins. Mechanistic piety is the price for spiritual objectivity. As the passion for detail turns into an obsession, the Jewish world is liable to compulsive neuroses. Rabbis and congregations chase after the ingredients of glue on postage stamps, the oil in sardine tins, and kosher kiss-proof lipsticks. Serious gatherings consider the levitical impurity caused by the mummified body of Jeremy Bentham in University College, London. Only humour and holy jokes save the Jewish world from the ridiculous. Heresy and fanaticism are the result of too logical minds, and humour is the best antidote.

Liturgy is usually too grand for jokes. Its creators do not like to mix their genres, for too many weak points are revealed. Occasionally in the Jewish liturgy, rabbis have had enough courage and sanity to let jokes peep in, surrounded by the thanksgivings and psalms of the people. At Passover, a parody of rabbinic exegesis is used to inflate the number of plagues which God sent on Egypt. The parody inflates the plagues but it also deflates the nationalism inherent in the story. Parody also occurs at Purim – the feast of Esther. Three rabbis would come to the front of the synagogue, constitute themselves a Jewish court with binding authority, and proceed to decide with the full rabbinic apparatus and expertise comic questions posed by the congregation.

In a world where religion is judicial, and judges have great authority, this keeps the inhabitants humble. By this gateway they come to self-awareness.

Christians and Jews are taught the same virtues, but by very different means. A Jew seeks humility, not by falling on his knees but by self-deflation in a joke, soul-searching is similarly replaced by alienation. He sees himself with ironic detachment, reflected in many cultural mirrors, and the result is not dissimilar.

This objectivity and detachment of religion also affects the way Jews approach things which lie at the heart of religion. God is not dependent on their feelings and a gulf separates them. This distance helps Jews to view the workings of the Almighty with a certain clarity, and acceptance. It is not assumed that He has arranged the Cosmos to fit in with personal demands, or that the power of creation can fit into a human image. In prayer, Jews stand upright facing God. They have their own position, and standing. The distance, which at first seems chilling, enables Jews to be themselves, and the Almighty to be Himself as well. The distance is necessary for freedom so that they do not suffocate each other.

In the centre of Christianity is a cross. It is at the centre of all Christian religious paths, and roads. Suffering conquered and transcended is a highway which leads to God. In Judaism it is not there. Joy and suffering, pain and pleasure, all lead to a knowledge of God's will, and it is both human and legitimate to avoid the more painful paths to awareness, if this can possibly be done. In fact it would be considered silly to do anything else. Austerities and penances exist on the fringes of present-day Judaism, but an atmosphere of suspicion surrounds them. Only the small residue which pass all psychiatric tests, and are well pickled in tradition, are allowed grudgingly through the religious doors.

This does not mean that Jews have any illusion as to the balance of pleasure and pain in human life. On the contrary, Judaism assumes that there is a considerable amount of the latter. In fact there is so much of it from the outside, that the task of religion is not to increase it by adding internal sufferings. Its task is to reduce the preoccupation with suffering, in order that the people may remain sane, and keep their balance. The greatness of Judaism does not lie in transcending suffering, but in reducing it to proportion. From experience, Judaism ought to put a cross at the centre of its faith. It does not, because this would mean a distortion of its task, which is to build God's Kingdom in a chaotic world, and be His prisoners of hope.

The last war brought Christians and Jews together. The former experienced a deep wave of feeling for their Jewish brethren, who had gone through the experience of a crucifixion. They saw Jews in an apocalyptic light, and the inferno of the holocaust led directly to the epic rise of a Jewish state. Their gaze turned from the concentration camps to Israel, but in doing so they passed over a commonplace and very Jewish phenomenon. This is not surprising, because many Jews did the same, it was so matter-of-fact. All over Europe the remnants of communities, which had been decimated, re-formed themselves in the neighbourhood of the concentration camp sites, and laboriously tried to re-create the old life. The sufferings and the memories were locked away. These little 'survivor' communities seemed so normal, but even to appear ordinary in this situation, meant a stoic heroism. Only when Judaism is understood from within, does this unsensational strength and purpose reveal itself.

There is always a joke, which illustrates the great features of Jewish experience. It was announced in Tel Aviv that God was going to send a tidal wave thirty-feet high over the city because of its sins. Muslims went to their mosques to pray for a speedy translation to the paradise of the prophet. Christians went to their churches to pray for the intercession of the saints, but the Jews went to the synagogues and prayed, 'Lord God, it's going to be difficult living under thirty feet of water!'

For centuries Jewish life has been lived under emergency conditions. The enemy has not been an internal one, a Satan eating his way through the people's moral fibre, but an external one. Every so often the alarm is sounded, the refugee lines form and the people pack up and go. There is neither the time, nor the room, to take very much with them. They pack what they can into their suitcases, and take the first train out to another culture, if they are lucky enough to get an entry visa. They are the refugees of Brecht, who 'have to change their country more often than their shoes'. After all the centuries the old pattern is still there. They are still a group of wandering Aramaeans, fleeing from another Pharoah and being led to another appointment with the Transcendent.

Adaptability, not rigidity, is a religious requirement in this situation. They cannot afford too many memories, because they would drown in them. Every Jewish family has its store of souvenirs, perhaps from a village in Russia before the Revolution, a pre-1933 café in Berlin or Vienna, a house in Alexandria, the memories of other towns and cultures they have passed *en route*. Time and again Jews turn back to remembrance of things past – Proust was Jewish too! Yiddish accents, expensively eradicated through private schooling, suddenly reappear, someone hums a sentimental tune about a Yiddishe Momma, and a wave of nostalgia threatens to engulf all present. This nostalgia has stolen into popular songs and dance music, and every so often the entire world turns to Jewish memories, and weeps for a Momma they have never known, and tries with the Jews to sing the Lord's song in a strange land.

This is just an escape valve. Yet there is always a danger that it will become something more – a prison with memories, locking Jews in, and turning them away from reality, work and God's purpose. This is part of the price that is paid for being 'the people of God'. This phrase, which looks so attractive, was very popular at the second Vatican Council, with other phrases like 'pilgrim church' on earth. The consequences are not so appealing. Christians would be well advised to look at the Jewish experience, and learn the cost of the journey.

It means tying oneself to a power which moves people on from country to country, and culture to culture. It means being homeless in history, and geography too. It means giving up settled conditions and permanence. The journey needs, above all, shrewdness and adaptability to stand upright in the changes. It needs a sense of humour to overcome insecurity, and the bitterness it can bring. Since the 'people of God' cannot be martyrs all the time, everywhere, they have to camp down where they can. They have to try and live as cosily as they dare with this immense will, which drags them from deserts to affluent suburbs, and from there to concentration camps.

The remnants of the middle ages died in the last war, and the mentality they produced is fading away with the forms of medieval piety. Strange changes have taken place. For the first time for millennia Judaism is the established religion of a state, and Christians have to make requests to a Jewish Ministry of Religious Affairs. For Christians the order has changed as well. The attitudes of the Council of Trent look strange in a secular world, and only raise a smile in the Communist East – an anachronism of history, which has parted company with reality. Christians turn to an older image, which suits their present situation more. They realise again that they are the 'people of God' travelling through real history, not a series of temptations, a pilgrim church on earth. Life on the road brings the two religions together, or at least closer for they are both God's gypsies. The Jews have a great deal to tell about the dangers and joys of this road, the lore one must know, what can be carried along, the qualities such a life requires, the tolls one has to pay, the holy compromises and the accommodations that have to be made, and how one feels towards a Master who sends us out on such journeys.

Chapter Eight

Arguing One's Way to Heaven

Lord of the universe, You are doing much to make me desert my faith, but I assure You that, even against the will of the dwellers in heaven, a Jew I am and a Jew I shall remain; and neither the sufferings that You have brought upon me nor that which You will yet bring upon me will be of any avail.

Solomon Ibn Verga

> Good morning to You, Almighty God,
> I, Levi Yitzhok son of Sarah of Berditchev,
> Have come for a judgment against You,
> On behalf of Your People Israel.
> What do You want of Your people Israel?
> The slightest thing, and You say,
> 'Speak to the children of Israel'.

Rabbi Levi Yitzhok

Judaism is a noisy religion. The faithful are rarely silent. Hosea said 'Take with you words', and this commandment at least has been well kept. And as if their mouths are not enough, Jews also use their hands as they speak, argue and discuss. They do this with each other, and they do the same with God.

Jews even study divine law traditionally in pairs, so that they can argue better. How can one argue with oneself? Many feel uneasy with this vehement approach to religion. Surely God, they say, should be sought in silence, head reverently bowed, mind an inviting blank, eyes reverently closed. How can one seek the Divine in the atmosphere of a holy prizefight? Yet this is the meaning of the name Israel, 'one who struggles with God'. It was not given to Jacob after quiet meditation, but after prolonged and realistic struggle with a messenger of God; Jews, even in their religion, assert the human-ness of humans; the arguing, contradictory, passionate side to our nature that God put in us. We are not holy vegetables, bits of religious asparagus, quietly growing upwards, complying with divine requirements, in a dull earthy silence.

An argument is not something to shy away from, an embarrassment to the search for holiness. It might seem vulgar, but the prophets and martyrs were too passionate to be gentlemen, and never raise their voices. Provided the conditions are right one can argue one's way through to God Himself. This is in fact one of the paths to holiness which is specially Jewish. It influences the outlook of Jews, the way they think, and also incidentally contributes to the humour of the secular world. Argument and bargaining are not new in the religious search – they exist in the earliest Hebrew religious traditions, and the holiest and deepest at that.

Abraham does not merely pray to God passively, begging the Almighty, he bargains with Him, arguing with the same intensity for the fate of the men of Sodom as any stall-holder in a Jewish market. The difference (and it is a very important one) is that he is not arguing for himself. The argument never dries up. Balaam argues with his ass, Moses argues with the Children of Israel, the Children of Israel argue with each other, and with their Creator. He is, after all, their father, not a stranger, and like all children they argue with Him. They cry from time to time that 'it's not fair'. If there is intimacy and trust, such things can be done. It is much more natural, and more pious than putting God under a theological microscope, dissecting Him like a demonstration guinea-pig, with a detachment which is remote from the free play and intimacy of real love.

A lovely example of this holy argument is found in the book of Hosea. There God is about to divorce His people for adultery. The prophet pleads the case for the defence. He draws on his own experience, which was not inconsiderable, as he was married to a harlot. Another example of Jewish argument is found in the

Talmud. Since it is given laconically and no conclusions are drawn, I give it as it appears in Baba Metzia, a tractate of the Talmud. The reader can draw his own conclusions I merely draw attention to the key statements made in this tussle between the rabbis and the Almighty, so that their strangeness and depth should not be passed over.

On a certain occasion R. Eliezer used all possible arguments to substantiate his opinion, but the rabbis did not accept it. He said, 'If I am right, may this carob tree move a hundred yards from its place'. It did so . . . They said, 'From a tree no proof can be brought'. Then he said, 'May the canal prove it'. The water of the canal flowed backwards. They said, 'Water cannot prove anything'. Then he said, 'May the walls of this House of Study prove it'. Then the walls of the house bent inwards, as if they were about to fall. R. Joshua rebuked the walls, and said to them, 'If the learned dispute about the Law, what has that to do with you?' So, to honour R. Joshua, the walls did not fall down, but to honour R. Eliezer, they did not become straight again. Then R. Eliezer said, 'If I am right, let the heavens prove it.' Then a heavenly voice said, 'What have you against R. Eliezer? The Law is always with him.' Then R. Joshua got up and said. 'It is not in heaven' (Deut 30 : 12). What did he mean by this? R. Jeremiah said, 'The Law was given us from Sinai. *We pay no attention to a heavenly voice.* For already from Sinai the Law said, "By a majority you are to decide" ' (Exodus 23 : 2, as homiletically interpreted). R. Nathan met Elijah and asked him what God did in that hour. Elijah replied, '*He laughed* and said, "My children have conquered".'

It is important in our time that this argument in tradition should continue inside the search for holiness, and be accepted within the tradition. Religious acceptance comes at the end, but one cannot cheat one's way there with a false passivity. It is spontaneous, natural, and right to protest at the suffering which falls on oneself or on another. So much of it seems unmerited, unhelpful, and inconsequential. For a Jew it is not right just to endure persecution and concentration camps. He was given a mouth to ask, and limbs to act. Only when protest and action have been tried, and the argument has been pursued to the deepest level, can he afford to give up with decency, and accept God's will with resignation.

It is sometimes forgotten how Jewish Jesus was in all his reactions. In the garden, he did not take the cup of suffering and bitterness without question. We do not know exactly what was said, and how much was expressed aloud, but we are left with a few significant words. 'Father take this cup from me . . . nevertheless not as I will but Thou wilt.' There too is the sign of argument and struggle for no Jew can ever be God's robot. He was not created to be a religious automaton, or a human prayer wheel. He has to assimilate God's command into himself, and this means argument at the deepest level of his being. Holy argument is the greatest path to God in Jewish experience, and dialectic is as effective for a Jew as a rosary is for a catholic, in approaching the Almighty.

God has never stopped talking to His people, and His people have never stopped answering back – rather like a conversation on a 'walkie-talkie' or two-way radio. The Bible is part one of the argument, and the Talmud is part two, even more argumentative than its predecessor. It is so very argumentative in fact, that many Jews take fright when they first dip into it. It depends what you want from a religious book, and what form you desire from a religious search. For the Talmud is not a book of holy conclusions, it is a book of holy arguments. The argument wanders through volume after volume of this vast work. Rabbis argue with each other, so do the generations, and the Almighty argues with Himself. The path to heaven is noisy with discussion and holy discord. Occasionally all the parties, rabbis, the generations, and the Almighty Himself pause for breath as it were, and a holy conclusion is born. But there is a certain reluctance to do this. Reality forces decisions on us, the world breaks in, and the holy argument is regretfully stopped, before all its religious potential has been used. The argument does not exist for a conclusion, it exists in its own right, as a way of purification. If you argue properly, you purify your mind and your passions.

The schools of Shammai and Hillel argued on every point in

the years before Jesus, and the arguments between them vibrate through the early centuries of the Talmud. Which was right? God didn't seem to be of much help. 'The views of these', He said 'and the views of these, are the words of the living God'. For practical purposes, however, He indicated Hillel. So it is with many decisions in life. It is the way we approach them, not the conclusions that matter. Do we wish to sit, or do we wish to stand? Both states have their advantages and their disadvantages. Because one is chosen, the other is not wrong. In Jewish law, the rejected line is not necessarily heretical. It may well flower at a future time.

A marriage dispute came before a rabbi, he heard the wife patiently. 'You are right,' he said. The husband intervened, and the rabbi listened to him, and considered carefully. 'You are right, too,' he said. A bystander shouted out, 'If she's right, how can he be right?' The rabbi pondered. 'And you're right too', he exclaimed. If you have Jewish ears you will hear, and a Jewish mind you will understand. Judaism does not speak in the language of Greek logic, its message is given in the flexibility of the 'mashal' – the parable, and its secrets lie at the heart of jokes.

Even a self-respecting card-player knows that the quality of the game is more important than who wins. If this is so, in cards, how much the more so in religion, when the symbols are those of eternal life. When you understand this, you will be able to read the Talmud. You will understand why rabbis loved pursuing God's will into bizarre and improbable territory, and only partly in fun, for the pursuit is as important as the result. You will be tempted to give up, but before you turn to more pious books, think about arguments and conclusions. Think also about the people in the Talmud who argued. They were doctors, and lawyers, and administrators, and many of them died for these arguments with bravery and devotion. A Zen master might see beneath the surface easily, to the hidden point of this seeming pointlessness.

Rabbis have argued as to whether a self-winding watch can be worn on the Sabbath. Does a ritual booth (which has to be open to the sky) and which is built under a stationary Zeppelin, fulfil a person's obligation? If a man writes a divorce on a leaf, is it valid? If a drop of milk falls into a meat soup, can the result be eaten? Endless erudition and piety have been poured into such matters.

Should the Shema – the great Jewish prayer – be always recited before going to bed? The Torah itself does seem to say so. Yet, Rabban Gamliel declared, not on a man's marriage night. A sensible decision, as a man would not be able to say the prayer properly. His mind could not possibily be on the job. Can one ever tell a lie? Not really, but there are rare occasions where it is permissible. When you go to a wedding, always tell the groom how lovely his bride is. But, it was objected, what if she has a beard? Tell him still! And what if he married her for money? It makes no difference, tell him still how lovely his bride is. Jewish Law and paralysed ethics are not the same thing.

There is a great danger, of course, that this path to religious awareness can become a game of refined acrostics. Expertise of the mind can replace the piety of the heart. This has happened from time to time in Judaism, and waves of popular mysticism and spirituality have risen as protest movements from the common people, because they were spiritually undernourished, and sometimes starved. But the path of argument and dialectic has many inbuilt safeguards and refinements. Its intellectual integrity has stood the Jewish world in good stead, and has been its strength. Some minutes before the German invasion of Lithuania in 1940, the rabbi of the great Talmudic college there gave this speech. The dignity of the scribes and Pharisees had settled on their disciple!

'With the full weight of the authority granted to me as your Rabbi, I command you to leave me here. You must flee and save yourselves! Take heed of your bodies and your souls. Do not place your lives in danger unnecessarily because of the lightning bolt that strikes from without, but do not think for one fleeting instant that you must sacrifice your lives for inner spiritual matters. I beseech and adjure you to remember always those of our people who fell at the hands of the murderers. My dear students, always remember the Nehardea of Lithuania, the Yeshiva of Slabodka. And when the world returns again to stability and quiet, never become weary of teaching the glories, the wisdom, the Torah and the Musar [i.e. the law and discipline of Lithuania], the beautiful and ethical life which Jews lived here. Do not become embittered by wailing and tears. Speak of these matters with calmness and serenity, as did our holy Sages. And so as our holy Sages have done – pour forth your words and cast them into letters. This will be the greatest retribution which you can wreak upon these wicked ones. Despite the raging wrath of our foes the holy souls of your brothers and sisters will then remain alive. These evil ones schemed to blot our names from the face of the earth; but a man cannot destroy letters. For words have wings; they mount up to the heavenly heights and they endure for eternity.'

The greatness of study came from the purification which accompanied it. It was this which made the argument and study holy. Without it study becomes mere cleverness, and falls into the same traps as the modern Ph.D. industry. The warning is contained in the earliest writings of the Talmud. Study of the Torah, it says, must not be used as a spade to dig with, nor as a crown to crown yourself with. It must be done for its own sake. Time and time again through tractate after tractate the words 'for its own sake' are used. This was the great defence against using religion for ambition and vanity – a dangerous mixture.

The lessons of this extend far beyond religion. The modern world is as preoccupied with argument and study as the rabbinic world, and there is a boom in cleverness. The ingenious monkey side to our nature is given every encouragement, but little discipline. The result is that enormous power is placed in the hands of the immature, and technology in the service of the unpurified instincts. Bombs are literally put into the hands of children.

This purification prevented knowledge becoming a technique

for manipulating others. Knowledge of the Talmudic type required self-awareness. The scope of Talmudic knowledge was always more than awareness of the external world but of the inner world as well. But it did not fall into the trap of making a complete distinction between the observer and the observed. The terms of modern analytical psychology were, of course, not known, but the facts they described were. It was well known that if the work did not go on within as well as without, all the cleverness would result in projecting inner hangups on to the external world. At the present moment, it is possible to buy an ideology for the price of a paper-back, which can justify all childish aggressions. This kind of knowledge does not liberate and make people free, the 'cleverness' locks them and imprisons them still further into their own limitations.

For Pharisaic Judaism study and prayer were so closely allied that they seemed little more than two sides of the same coin. It was a matter of debate if the greatest prayer should be studied or prayed. The place of worship could be called indifferently synagogue or school. This meant that study was not done for material advantage. Like prayer, it was done in the presence of God, and in the service of God. Its rewards were not degrees or titles or money, but the refinement of the personality and the spirit. Is it stupid to work without reward? Does it get one anywhere? To many people in present-day society, it would be stupid. To rabbis the alternative would have seemed more stupid.

At the beginning of the morning prayers the following passage is traditionally said, while the worshipper's eyes are still heavy with sleep. This is the sacrifice of study, which is made to God.

Rabbi Ishmael says: 'There are thirteen exegetical principles by which the law is expounded :

1. The inference from minor to major.
2. The inference from a similarity of phrases.
3. The general law may be derived by induction from different cases which, occuring in the same or in different verses, have yet some feature in common.
4. A general proposition followed by the enumeration of par-

ticulars already comprehended in the general proposition (in which case the scope of the proposition is limited by the things specified) . . .'

The aim of Jewish study was not really the knowledge of God. That was too daring. It was not expected that any beatific vision would come to the intellect, or that it would be possible to take degrees in religious experience. Theology was not at the heart of religion, nor did the rabbis make the nineteenth-century mistake of equating piety with culture. The aim of Jewish study was not to experience God, but to know His will. The former is after all a pleasure, but the latter is duty and work. 'Law, commandments, statutes, and ordinances' are the daily bread of any society, holy or otherwise. Philosophy is the decoration. As a religion Judaism was temperamentally closer to the attitudes of Martha than to those of Mary.

The subject matter of Jewish study was the world, but great care was taken that study did not become worldly. There is a difference between the old rabbinic universities, the yeshivot, and their modern secular equivalents. To take an example – the former were as carefully sited as the latter, but not in any pre-possessing area. The surroundings were meant not to distract, and they can be found in unattractive countryside, or in run-down suburbs of industrial towns. Study was regarded as an act of faith, in which one stripped oneself. It was an act of concentration, and an act of giving. Many student demonstrations today are conformist in a deep sense. The dispute with society is not over its basic materialism, because this is shared. The dispute concerns how the spoil is divided, and how soon the protesters can enter into the bourgeois inheritance. It is a difference concerning the distribution of loot, not any real discussion concerning its existence. Occasionally ideology, or charitable donations, are used as fig-leaves to hide this nakedness, but the basic greed, which the 'haves' and the 'have nots' share, is obvious.

Against this, the Talmud gives another picture of student life, which would seem foolish if one did not know what was at stake :

'This is the way of Torah! A piece of bread with salt you

will eat, a ration of water you will drink, upon the ground you will lie, a life of hardship you will lead, and you will labour in the Torah. If you do this 'happy shall you be' – in this world. 'And it shall be well with you' – in the world to come.'

The aim of study was to marry reality with religion – not to restrict religion to piety, but to find the will of God in relation to life as it was lived. The detail was mountainous, the arguments exhaustive, and the quietness of religion seems far away. The Talmud is not a book to put beside one's bed for religious refreshment. It is not a book of beautiful thoughts. It is a continuing argument about civil and criminal law, far more concerned with property rights, penalties and legal damages than with souls and their salvation.

This marriage of religion and reality was so well done that it remained in force for nearly two millennia, obeyed and kept by Jews almost without exception. When the enlightenment came, all the inhabitants of the Ghetto had to do was to turn their eyes from their old religious books on to the new secular ones. They approached modern knowledge with the same passion with which their grandparents had approached the Talmud, and Jewish Law. The blaze of Jewish intellect in modern times, the tremendous heritage it has given to the entire world in the nineteenth and twentieth centuries would have surprised the scribes and Pharisees. It would have seemed so narrowly materialist in their eyes. Nevertheless, this was their last gift to the world, and all who benefit from Jewish discoveries in science, or take pleasure in Jewish art, and the great modern literature Jews have produced, are in debt to the Scribes and Pharisees.

Chapter Nine

Revelation in the Newspaper

Give me your tired, your poor,
Your huddled masses yearning to breathe free,
The wretched refuse of your teeming shore,
Send these, the homeless, tempest-tost, to me,
I lift my lamp beside the golden door.
                    Emma Lazarus (Poem on the Statue of Liberty)

From each according to his abilities, to each according to his needs.
                    Karl Marx

May His Kingdom come in your lifetime, and in your days, and in the
lifetime of all the family of Israel – quickly and speedily may it come.
                    Kaddish (An Aramaic prayer in the liturgy)

Jews are passionate politicians. In the world of the Jewish immigrants to the West, the remnants of which can still be seen in
East London or New York, religious life is interwoven with the
strands of Marxism, socialism, anarchism, and every other pro-
gramme for the betterment of man. Jews hurled themselves into
the Spanish Civil War, or in their innocence returned to the
Soviet Union, and were never heard of again. This combination
of religious and political utopianism is sporadic in Christianity,
but endemic in Judaism. This is why Jews get into so much
trouble, because they are always trying to put perfection into the
world, and burning their fingers in the process. Israel is an
example. It cannot be just an ordinary state, although the existence of that would be hard enough. It must be the perfect
state, the state which is an example, and which teaches other

people how to run their own. This must be intensely irritating to anyone who lives in the vicinity, which few Jews realise. Israel is also interesting because of another peculiarity : people there read more newspapers than anywhere else. Newspapers are not merely read, they are studied. The journals of political parties are treated like religious texts.

In fact this is what they are! They could be put beside holy writings, because if they are read in the right way, they provide a revelation of the Almighty. Jews are not only the people of the Book, they are also the people of many books, and weeklies, and monthlies, and dailies too. Traditionally, of course, there were useless books. I once had a discussion, and it was not in jest, as to what books one was permitted to read in the most private room in a Jewish house – the john – the Law is, after all, capable of dealing with all contingencies. It was quite clear that Law and codes were out, but what about studying someone said the 'wars of gentile kings', even though in medieval literature this was classified as light. As most Jewish life has had to adapt to their whims and cruelties, it seemed a reasonable enough suggestion. It was considered and rejected. It was of no benefit – like the weather, gentile kings had to be endured. Like women's gossip such affairs were outside the sphere of rational interest. The rabbis present, after some debate, recommended Maimonides and his *Guide to the Perplexed!* Jews were not commanded to be philosophers or theologians.

What is holy in the newspaper then, if it is not the wars of gentile kings, or women's gossip? There is, after all, very little left! Jews have a normal interest in such matters, but their attention is really absorbed when they read about their fellow Jews, and what is happening to them. Now this is not just ordinary parochialism, it is also the result of a deep-seated religious attitude. God reveals Himself in His dealings with His people. There, if one can interpret it, is a revelation of God's essence, appearing in communal magazines, and Jews read them avidly.

Religion is not just piety, and it was certainly not so for the prophets. Jeremiah specialised in foreign affairs, and most had something to say about the politics, both internal and external of the people. Their concerns were deeply political, and included land speculation, profiteering, foreign policy, debt and inflation. This prophetic tradition was continued by the Pharisees. It would have been stupid for them to talk about the great affairs of state, for unlike the prophets they had no state. The Jews were just starting their social descent, to become the pariah people of the middle ages. Nevertheless they carried on the same interests. What was the will of God, they asked, in small civil matters? These were important, for here the Law could still be implemented. Rabbis were interested in what they could implement, and in what they could change. They were not just pastors of communities, and they were certainly not priests, but they were the religious mayors, God's judges, and His police force. They knew no distinction between secular and religious, their distinction lay in what was practical and what was not.

The Torah is a kind of blueprint of a holy and righteous society, and Judaism in all its forms is devoted to building it, whether in the microcosm of the suburb and the ghetto, or in the macrocosm of the Jewish state. At no time is anyone exempt. Even in Theresienstadt, Jews organised themselves as rationally as they could, and rabbis such as Leo Baeck gave lectures on Hellenic influences on Judaism. Society had to be kept going at all costs with such blessings of culture as were available. The legal answers of the rabbis of Poland before the destruction of the ghetto showed how seriously this task was taken. Dominant themes were suicide, and the weighing of lives in times of peril. Here too the will of God could and had to be discovered by rational means, and implemented as Jewish Law had always been implemented, by its moral force, and the love and loyalty it generated.

Many realities doubtless exist. Pharisaic Judaism has always asserted this, but only 'the world has He given to the children of men'. What God does with us in other worlds is His business – His religion if you like – but the upkeep of this world, our world, is our business as long as we are in it. 'One moment of good deeds and repentance in this world is finer than all the life of the world to come' says the Talmud; although it understandably adds that 'one moment of bliss in the world to come is worth more than all this world has to offer'. It depends on where you are – that is all!

Jews then are preoccupied by society out of a religious demand. Even when the religious belief has died, the demand continues in the minds of Jews, influencing them even in their secular concerns. They do not know it, but the word of God has gone much deeper into them than they thought. The majority of those who applied to join the Peace Corps in the United States were Jews, though they form only a very small percentage of the population. When asked about their motives, the applicants overwhelmingly denied that religion had anything to do with it. The striking characteristic of Judaism today is the power it still commands, and the ignorance and unawareness of those whom it influences.

This explains why Jews read newspapers but it does not explain why they enjoy them. Many people come to religion through fear. Most of us do in one way or another, for love usually appears later on the scene. Whenever the Stock Market goes down there is a tendency towards the contemplative life. Some years ago I took the Day of Atonement Services after a financial shock. The intensity of interest and devotion were gratifying. The liturgy said that the world was dust, and that no man could be relied on. There was complete agreement among the worshippers, who nodded vigorously. Their accord became even more pronounced, as I talked about the frailty of man, the impermance of earthly things, and the bliss of the world to come, where nothing fades, nothing rusts, and prospectuses are presumably reliable. Being Jews, I knew that the fascination of the hereafter would be short-lived, for the tide of Judaism carries its people to the religious demand of the here. Rabbis take their chance when they can to ram transcendence home.

For others the fascination of the hereafter is not short-lived. Religion is seen as a way in which time can be transcended or stopped. 'Stop the world, I want to get off!' is a modern catchphrase, and religion is a way of getting off. I do not mean this cynically, and I am not saying that religion of this type is escapism. God does lie beyond time, and time can certainly be an obstacle, and get in the way. By prayer we come to realities, which are not subject to time, and with this detachment we can act in the world. We have stepped out of time, and into eternity.

But for a Jew this cannot be done, because it is also stepping out of God's revelation to us. It is trying to escape the dimension He puts us in, avoiding its reality, and feel, and the impulses He sends through it. The beauty of music, and the glory of revelation can only exist in time – time is their essence. There are folk proverbs that time is a healer, but for Jews it is even more – it is holy.

Without it, Jews could never know what God is like. The universe around us is frightening in its vastness, its prodigality, and its indifference. How do we come to a benevolent creator in this vast emptiness, dotted with rock and fire. At best it seems indifferent to us, at worst hostile. Christians, as they seek the face of God, turn from the vastness around them to the sufferings of Christ. Jews too, need something more than nature, something more intimate than 'the heavens, the work of My hands', in order to live with integrity, and without bitterness. They seek God's face in the history of their people. His character so to speak is revealed not only at Mount Sinai but in the story of His dealings with Jews. And the story has not yet ended. It is found in the holy writings of past times, and in the chronicles of the present. The Torah is a book of law within a book of history. The law is set in time, and moves through time. Time is the instrument, by which God shapes and refines it.

Jews and Christians have the same Ten Commandments, but they number them differently. In the Jewish division the first commandment is not 'Thou shalt have no other Gods before me', but 'I am the Lord thy God who brought thee out of the land of Egypt, out of the house of bondage'. Now this is not exactly a commandment, but unless it is accepted, none of the other commandments stand. After all, anybody can tell us to do anything. How do we know the nature and goodwill of the One who gave them? Because of the exodus, the rabbis said. But for Him the

97

people would have no existence. It is He who gave us freedom, dignity, and whatever greatness we possess. Through His actions in time, we know Him sufficiently to trust Him, even when it goes against our instincts, and our nature. When a Jew commences the celebration of the Sabbath he blesses the day. This, he says, is a remembrance of the creation, i.e. it is the birthday of the world, and therefore of time. It is also the remembrance of the creation of our people in history. And at the end of the Sabbath, prayers and songs are recited for the coming of God's Kingdom in time. The imminence of its coming, is even stated – 'in your lifetime, and in the days of the Jewish people', 'soon may He come with the Messiah, the son of David'.

It is said that at the time of the Reformation the Calvinist envoys came to Luther and spoke to him concerning the kingdom of God on earth, for the time was right. Luther, who believed that time had been transcended, was angry, and threw them out, shouting *'Opiniones Judaici!'* And in this, at any rate, he was very right. It was a very Jewish thought, and a very Jewish impulse. It explains why Calvinists have usually understood Jews, and felt a bond between them. The essence of the dispute is the holiness of time.

This is what keeps Judaism going – its essential hopefulness about time. Judaism is like an old and battered car bearing the dents of many collisions. Yet the engine never seems to wear out, and it is a very powerful one indeed, because it uses messianic fuel. The steering may be erratic, but the journey never lacks speed, vitality, and optimism. Like Toad of Toad Hall the open road of history beckons us on, and just over the horizon, in the recognisable world, is the end of our struggle and strife.

It is the newspaper which separates Judaism from Christianity, and makes it chary of other worldliness. Bluntly stated, the Jew looks at his newspaper, and asks himself, as he looks at the murders, the demonstrations, the fear, and the falsity, 'Is this a picture of a redeemed world?' In his mind are the pictures of the Old Testament, the times of peace and progress the old men sitting under their vine trees, the wedding processions going through Jerusalem, the security, and the justice. The Christian would, of course, answer, that the seeds of God's kingdom are already here, the transformation has already begun, and the redemption has taken place in the hearts of believers. But the Torah and Jewish tradition do not point to an interior world. They speak of a world of external acts. The laboratory is mankind and the heart of man, but the end of the commandments is a result in the external world.

Jews, of course, know and have learnt from bitter experience, that unless there is an inner purification and a refinement of motives, external acts are themselves falsified, and a disease will exist in any utopia based upon them. In fact none of the societies and states Jews have built has lasted. It was not only a hostile external world which destroyed them, but an inner failing also, of prejudice, of dishonesty, and misunderstanding. This is never avoided either by the prophets or the rabbis. The statement of it is indeed the greatest glory of the Jewish people. They were willing to canonise their own self-criticism, and arrange for every Jew to expose himself to it weekly. It is, after all, not easy to sit through the prophetic passages in a synagogue service. There are too many parallels between the Jewish predicament now and the Jewish predicament then to be comfortable.

Modern re-writing of history by nations to excuse themselves, or suppress the evidence is childish and primitive. The self-criticism of the prophets and Pharisees is searing. After the defeat by the Romans, the Pharisees made no attempt to pass the buck, 'because of our sins', says the Jewish liturgy 'we were exiled from our land'. Our sins, not their sins! Jerusalem was destroyed, the Talmud says, because the people in the city did not treat each other decently.

The raw material of revelation is found in the newspaper, but to interpret it one must be free of individual or collective vanity. Politics are heady stuff. Nationalism especially is a great distorter, because it involves so much pride with few safeguards against megalomania or fantasies of grandeur. The student thinks he manipulates, whereas in fact he himself is manipulated by tides of ego. To understand and to interpret requires a detachment and a simplicity which go to the heart. Both Judaism and

Marxism share this concern for the newspaper and for history. For both the greatest things have not yet come, and the best is still to be. For Christians and Moslems God has, so to speak, shown His hand.

In the confrontations over Russian Jewish immigrants and the exasperated exchanges between Israelis and Russians, the differences between Marxists and Jews are obvious, but the similarities are not. Both believe in themselves. Both are an integral part of European culture and neither accept a partial responsibility for the European tragedies of the last decades. Both have had the experience of making new, complex, and collective societies work. Christians feel too much guilt to be politically effective, and Moslems have not yet produced a state which can provide and master its own technology. This inadequacy is felt neither by Jews, nor by Marxists. Communists still look forward to a world takeover, for the dream of the Communist Manifesto has never been given up, neither its messianism nor its universalism. Jews also have little doubt that they could run things better than their neighbours in the Middle East. They are not exactly colonists, but they are natural interferers. They are called imperialists, which they are not, but they do find it difficult to understand that other peoples might prefer their own chaos to an alien efficiency.

From Judaism have come two religions – Christianity and Islam. Its third and latest child has not been a religion, but an ideology – Marxism. Most Marxists would, of course, scoff at this. The similarities they would say are superficial. One is after all scientific, the other is not. It is true, the style of language, and the terminologies are different, but they are easily translated from one into another. What is the difference between the Kingdom of God and the republic of goodness?

Both have created, and run societies, though Marxists often forget this. The greatest thing which unites them is the newspaper. Both see a force, working itself out through events. For Jews this force can be conceived personally, can be said to have a will, and can be found within the perceiver. For Marxists it is not a metaphysical, but a scientific fact – the clumsiness is not in the terminology they use, but in their awareness and perception of the force. Both are materialisms, yet neither materialism is straightforward. At its best the philosophical materialism of Marx leads to an idealism in practice, which leaves Marxists proud, but somehow disturbed. Yet Judaism, classified along with religions like Christianity, often feels uncomfortable in such spiritual company. Rabbis, who are very concerned with community organisation, feel confused and guilty from carrying a burden of spirituality, which is not rightly theirs.

They do not feel at home in the external worlds either, for the external world is a very puzzling place. God has certainly spoken, but what has He said? What is the meaning of the destruction of European Jewry, and the rise of Israel? For Jews these are not just human affairs, to be given sociological explanations, which always look so neat after the event. These events are like the exodus, and the destruction of the Temple. A force has hurled Judaism into a new trajectory. It is not easy to say more.

Among ordinary Jewish people, interpretations are already taking place, without the help of intellectuals or rabbis. They are simple, potent, and possibly dangerous. For some the destruction of European Jewry was the punishment for assimilation, for being lured into the gentile world, for selling the Jewish inheritance, and birthright. For others, God took away six million dead, and Israel is the holy compensation. Jews are very sensitive about Israel. On its existence hinges the justice of God made visible in events. Some argue it is now proved that Jews should place no reliance on anyone but themselves; they should go it alone, so to speak. They point to the Jewish contribution to German culture. Their evidence is contained in a little encyclopaedia, called the *Philo Lexicon*, which was the last work German Jewry was allowed to publish. It could make no direct reply to the Nazis, all it could do was list the Jewish scientists, writers, musicians and artists of Germany and the German-speaking world. As the names succeed each other, Mendelssohn and Mahler, Freud and Einstein, Ehrlich and Wasserman, Kafka and Zweig, we realise it is a roll-call of German culture – a last post. It is strange now to read that Herzl, the founder of modern Zionism, advocated German as the language of the Jewish state, and said its purpose should be to spread German culture to the East. But there are others who argue the opposite, who say that now the Jewish problem is no more. It is only part of the world problem, and a human problem. They point to the later prophets, and the thread of universalism that runs through Judaism.

In Israel the problems of interpretation are vital. The Bible is not just a quarry for sermons, but a political textbook which in fact it always was. The Bible, however, is an argument which is never settled. Many threads run through it, and which is the vital one, which can illuminate modern Jewish history, and the nature of God? Should the political boundaries mentioned there be taken seriously – the empire extending from the Nile to the Euphrates? Should we listen instead to the prophet Jeremiah and others, who were willing to sacrifice political nationalism, for justice, sanity, and peace. These are living issues.

Behind them lies an even greater problem. Is the state messianic? Jews in Jerusalem asked the rabbinate if they could eat on the Black Fast, a day in the Jewish liturgical year, which commemorates past destructions, and which is supposed to disappear in the days of the Messiah. It is significant that despite the high-flown language Jews still fast, for the redemption has not come. The end is not yet in sight. When it came to a point of Jewish Law, the slogans abruptly ceased. All these questions run through Judaism. Something has been said, but who can interpret it for us? Bits of answers are everywhere. So Jews read newspapers avidly. Why did God allow so many to be killed? What should Israel do? Has God forsaken His people? The questions are infinite, different if Jews are born in Israel or outside, or from which of the seventy nations they come. The Jewish world is a small world. Every family has lost someone in the persecutions, and has a relative near the Israel frontiers. Passionately they want the answers. But where are they?

Hopefully, they buy another newspaper!

Chapter Ten

Towards the Unknown Country

On the dark path on which a man is to walk here on earth just as much light is provided as he wants for him to make the next step. More would only dazzle, and every side-light bewilders him.

Moses Mendelssohn

As the hand held before the eye hides the tallest mountain, so this small earthly life hides from our gaze the vast radiance and secrets of which the world is full, and whoever can take life from before his eyes, as one takes away one's hand, will see the great radiance within the world.

Chasidic

The truths of God are eternal, but Judaism is probably not. It is small in numbers, limited to a small people. It is also limited in time, because it is just a tool, an instrument of a power, which goes far beyond mankind, the world, the Cosmos, and whatever realities exist beyond that. It speaks of the will of God, but the will of God for a small nation. Whole areas of the will of God's work lie on its periphery, and there are sources of religious power and insight, which have found no place within it. It is committed to the words of the Torah, to build a society which will be a blessing to those within it, and bring a blessing to those outside it. It learns from its own children, from the spirituality of Christians, from the devotion of Moslems, and the immediacy of Marxists. Its claims have boundaries, but within those boundaries they are very deep.

For many people the integrity Judaism seeks is not enough. Something more is required – a deeper and more personal kinship with God as in Christianity, or a more profound apprehension of reality, as in the Eastern religions. The scribes and Pharisees were men of Law, who administered a little world, and respected its limits. One of them said to his pupils on his deathbed, 'May you fear God as much as you fear man!'. 'So little!' his pupils exclaimed. 'So much,' he answered.

So little is promised and expected, because what is promised must be kept. Pharisees and rabbis try to be honest with the Almighty. If ordinary civil law does not allow businessmen to cancel their contracts and specifications, how much the less could commitments to God be cancelled. The former would lead to chaos in the world of affairs, but the latter to a cosmic chaos, and the most dangerous of moral break-downs. The faithfulness of the despised world of business, the punctuality it demands, and the responsibilities it assumes, have much to teach religion. Rabbis never hesitated to learn from this world. Like all people who are lucky enough not to have too much, or too little, they had to earn their living in the cosmos. Neither God nor His universe owed them a living.

Such opinions, of course, are deeply unfashionable at a time when capitalism is losing confidence in itself and destroying itself through greed and cowardice. Yet there was a great attraction for Judaism in the bourgeois world, because it aimed at the possible, and because it was more interested in putting things up than in pulling them down.

The religion of the Pharisees has for centuries turned inwards to the Jewish world, because this is the situation that it has been set. It has not been able to ignore the outside world, because this is its God-chosen environment. If it is materialist in its concerns, it is because matter is a creation of God in its own right, with its own dignity, and not just a falling off from something else.

But despite all this, Jews have always known that beyond the small world of Judaism is a larger world, of which it is a microcosm, and beyond the world of men there is another, whose grandeur and bliss dwarf anything we know. The rabbis placed restrictions on the study of other realities, because such study could not benefit us until we were prepared for them, and knew how to treat them. Mysticism can, after all, easily become mystification and infinity can erode the painful distinctions built up over centuries between good and evil. Modern preoccupations with magic, astrology, and drug-induced experience show the reason for such caution. But the other worlds are there. To know this is fundamental to all Jewish understanding, just as not to be overwhelmed by them is fundamental to all Jewish practice.

The task of Judaism in fact is to tie knots, uniting one reality with others beyond; making the kitchen pots and pans, the doorways to the life of eternity. If Jewish life looks odd, filled with bizarre details and practices, it is because so many knots have been tied that the result may be a religious success, but it is certainly not an aesthetic one. But after all, the meat in the butcher's shop, and the clothes we wear, reveal God as well as ethics and poetry. He is just as present in awkward, clumsy, and ugly things as he is in the more obviously beautiful things, and in high-minded thoughts. The will of God exists for divorce as well as for marriage, and we bless Him in bad times as well as good (after all, what is the use of a good-time religion!). He is not for Judaism, the God of buttercups and daisies, and poetic sunsets. His nature is found in the laws concerning martyrdom, and the cases where anger is permissible.

The gates of the coming world are everywhere, if only one can see them. When I first went sailing, well-meaning friends tried to show me buoys, and beacons in the sea. I looked and saw nothing, while they saw beacons everywhere. As I did not know what to look for, I had no foretaste, no premonition of the sight. Therefore I could not see what all around me saw. Then I saw the first one, and suddenly the sea opened out. Buoys, cones, flashing lights, appeared everywhere. The empty sea seemed as crowded as Piccadilly Circus. So it is with Jewish life; every oddity, every departure from normal shows the tension, the effect in this world, when another which is far greater approaches it and disturbs it. It is like the disturbance in two heavenly bodies, as they approach each other – marks on the smaller reveal the force which the latter exerts as it comes nearer. These rules of Jewish Law, which seem so odd if we think of this world on its own, become understandable in relation to the existence of another world, and another reality.

This other reality surrounds and encloses the world in which Judaism works. To do our work, we have to know it is there, but we are not obliged to explore it. In past times the Law was the daily bread of Jewish life, normal, wholesome, comprehensible, and practical. The experience of this other world and the mysticism, contemplation, and speculation which led to it, were luxuries, cherries on the religious cake. Today the position is reversed. For many Jews the myriad details of the Law have become stranger and stranger in an open society, fitting in less and less with daily life, puzzling and inefficient. At the same time the urge to find a spiritual counterweight to the pressures of urban life has become stronger among Jews. Their strange mixture of secular precocity, and religious ignorance adds to the confusion. Out of all this comes a demand from the heart of the people. 'Demonstrate the reality of this other world! What is its meaning for our lives? Show us the reality of the unseen!'

This is the most urgent task for us today. The Law no longer leads to mysticism, but it is possible that mysticism may lead back to Law. Mysticism is an odd word, meaning many things. In Judaism it did not indicate a love affair with the Almighty. Such a state exists, but traditionally it is too intimate to discuss. Like one's love life and one's more intimate habits, it was private. Mysticism in its Jewish form, the Kabbalah, was an attempt to grasp the realities which came before and after our world, and which enfolded it. The pattern of Jewish prayers showed that we scarcely know things in themselves, we only know them polarised into their opposites in our experience. The aim of Jewish mysticism was to locate that reality, where all opposites come to unity.

In that country all things have their origin, the light and darkness, and the good and evil. Among the Kabbalists, charts are made of God and man, to find the source of that darkness. Every theory could exist, and the speculation of Jews has gone very far. For the Baal Shem Tov, God exists in all things, even in darkness, though our eyes cannot see Him. For Him evil can scarcely exist, it was a defect of our vision, our own limitation. Yet shortly after him, in the early nineteenth century, lived another rabbi, Nachman of Bratslav, who restated the Kabbalistic traditions and who turned away from the direction of pantheism to another extreme.

When God created the universe, he taught, He withdrew from a part of His own nature. The creation was therefore a catastrophic act of love, as well as a joy. God is therefore far. Sparks of His nature are scattered through creation, and it is our task to restore them to their holy source.

Such speculation in Judaism was for an inner circle, an esoteric elite. Scarcely one Jew in ten thousand has read or could read the Zohar, the work which sets out the Kabbalistic doctrines. The vast mass of Jews have not gone to heaven by this route. They have not denied its truth, but they have deliberately turned their eyes away to the small distinctions between the permitted and the forbidden and the little fences which separate the two. They did this so that the world should not fall apart. Our world is after all an in-between world, combining many levels of reality, and therefore unstable. It has to be handled with foresight and caution so that it does not break or blow apart. There is a rabbinic tradition that God created many worlds, but they all came to grief. The Pharisees and their pupils tried to ensure that this one did not go the same way.

This is not to say that they were entranced by this world, which they were not. It is recorded that they debated the existence of hell. They decided that it probably did not exist, but if it did this was it! This world was not a real resting place, it was just a corridor, a waiting room to another world. Yet the corridor had its own rules, and they had to be respected. Within these rules we were entitled to make ourselves as comfortable as possible. The Pharisees had no love for the Romans, who destroyed the Holy of Holies. They detested their policies, and their psychology, and regarded their own law as infinitely superior. But they gave them unstinting praise for their aqueducts and their roads. The evil inclination, they said, had its place, because it spurred men on to marry, to build houses and to compete, with it they built cities, and the structure of civilised life.

The corridor of course, leads to the door which is death. What is beyond it, is not dogmatically described. As one Pharisaic master reasonably said – no one has ever come back from there. Yet at the entrance to Jewish cemeteries are the Hebrew letters which stand for 'the house of life'. Although there is no formal doctrine of purgatory, death certainly did not break the laws of causation, or reward and punishment. It is typical of the Pharisees, that they pictured the Cosmos as a shop, a self-service store, in fact. Life was a kind of shopping expedition, with a party at the end. 'Everything is given on pledge, and a net is cast for all living. The shop is open, the shopkeeper gives credit, the account is open and the hand writes, and whoever wishes to borrow, may come and borrow, but the collectors go round every day, and exact payment from a man with his consent or without it, and their claims are justified, and the judgement is a judgement of truth. Yet everything is prepared for the feast!'

Moreover, there are no last rites in Judaism. There are certain prayers which should be said, and everyone is under an obligation to leave his affairs in order. Yet no passport is required to pass from the human world into God's domain. The awe of God is strong among Jews, but fear is rare. It is only pagans who do not know God's nature who have never felt His redemption in their history, who fear their own demons. The sign of the faithful is confidence. Death, original sin, and hell are not obsessive fears for Jews. Therefore the Christian message which brings release from all three is not immediately relevant to a Jewish situation. Such Jews as are attracted to the Christian message go there for other reasons.

Prometheus stole fire from the Gods. The Talmud has a different story. God provided men with the ability to make their own light, and find their own cure for their own fears. 'When Adam saw for the first time the sun go down, and an ever-deepening gloom enfold creation, his mind was filled with terror. God then took pity on him, and endowed him with the divine intuition, to take two stones – the name of one was darkness and the name of the other shadow of death – and rub them against each other, and so discover fire. Thereupon Adam exclaimed with grateful joy, "Blessed be the Creator of light!" '

So Jews try to earn their way to heaven, by patching up the world, and making it work. They have deliberately chosen religious prose, not because they could not write religious poetry, but because this was their service and their sacrifice. It is said that 'the lion shall lay down with the lamb'. Since Jews do not expect miracles, or pray for a change in the instincts of lions or lambs, it is a matter which requires thought and organisation. Someone, says one of the traditional commentators, will have to put a fence between them, and that someone will probably be a scribe or a Pharisee.

It was all summed up, long ago, by a contemporary of Jesus. Rabbi Tarphon says – 'The day is short, the work is great, and the labourers are sluggish, and the wages are high, and the Master of the house is insistent. It is not your duty to finish the work, but you are not free to neglect it. Faithful is your Employer to pay you the reward of your labours. But know that the reward of the righteous is in the time to come.'

Glossary

CHASSIDIC : A popular mystical movement which arose in Eastern Europe in the eighteenth century. Emphasised inner joy and prayer.

EL SHADDAI : A Biblical name for God. It designates Him as the 'Mysterium Tremendum', the God of Creation, and the God who inspires awe.

EIN SOF : Lit : 'the Endless', name used for the ultimate aspect of God which cannot be named.

GAON : Lit : 'excellence'. Originally given to principals of academies of Babylon. Later used as a special title for men of great scholarship and learning.

KABBALAH : Lit : 'tradition', used especially for the mystical, theosophic, and esoteric traditions in Judaism.

KARO : Rabbi Joseph Karo (1488–1575). Spanish scholar and mystic. Wrote the traditional code of Jewish Law.

KOSHER : Ritually clean and permitted. Used mainly today in connection with food.

LAO TSE : Chinese mystic and philosopher. Founder of Taoism (circa cighth century B.C.)

LADINO : Medieval Spanish dialect used by Jewish refugees from Spain. Spoken widely in the Eastern Mediterranean until the Nazi deportations.

MAIMONIDES : Rabbi Moses ben Maimon (1135–1204). Physician, philosopher, and jurist. Born in Spain, he lived in Cairo. Combined Aristotle and traditional Judaism.

MISHNAH : Part of the Talmud. Definitive oral law as laid down by Rabbi Judah the Prince.

MUSAR : Lit : 'discipline'. Ethical, legal and social school of religious thought in Lithuania in nineteenth century.

OLD TESTAMENT : Christian equivalent for Jewish 'Tenach' (see below).

RABBI : Post-biblical Jewish title with the meaning of 'my master'. Applied to Jesus. Indicates learning in the Law.

SHOOL : Yiddish for 'school'. Popular name for synagogue.

113

TALMUD : Lit : 'study'. The codification of the oral Law, together with the teachings and discussions, which took place in Palestine (The Jerusalem Talmud) and Babylon (The Babylonian Talmud), over a period of approx. 500 to 700 years.

TENACH : A word made up from the initial letters of the following : Torah (Pentateuch), Nevi'im (Prophets) and Khetuvim (writings). Equivalent to Christian usage of 'Old Testament'.

TEPHILLIN : Aids to prayer used in the morning to fulfil 'You shall bind them as a sign upon your hand, and they shall be reminders before your eyes' from Deuteronomy.

TORAH : The five books of Moses, the first five books of the Bible. Usually translated as 'law' but 'teaching' is more correct. Has come to mean all Jewish religious teaching.

YESHIVAH : Rabbinic college devoted to the study of the Law.

YIDDISH : Medieval German dialect carried by Jewish refugees to Eastern Europe at the time of the Crusades. Until the last war it was the language of the Jews who lived there or came from there. Written in Hebrew letters.

ZOHAR : Lit : 'brightness'. Main work of Spanish Jewish mysticism in the form of a commentary on the Torah, the Song of Songs, Ruth and Lamentations. End of thirteenth century.

DATE DUE

F 6/77			
MAR 16 '78			